More of
NATURE, NURTURE
and
NOSTALGIA

(Gleaned from the BLACK RIVER JOURNAL)

by

LOUIS MIHALYI

Artwork by
JOHN NORTON

Published by
North Country Books, Inc.
Utica, New York

More of Nature, Nurture and Nostalgia
Copyright © 1990

by
Louis Mihalyi

All rights reserved.
No part of this book may be reproduced
in any manner without the written permission of the author
except for brief quotes for review purposes.

Cover Art by John Norton

ISBN 978-0-932052-79-7

Library of Congress Cataloging-in-Publication Data

Mihalyi, Louis, 1921-
   More of nature, nurture, and nostalgia: gleaned from the Black River journal / by Louis Mihalyi: artwork by John Norton.
   p. cm.
   ISBN 0-932052-79-7:
   1. Natural history—New York (State) 2. Natural history—Northeastern States. I. Title.
QH105.N7M53   1990
507.747—dc20   89-71053
                                            CIP

Published by
North Country Books, Inc.
Publisher—Distributor
18 Irving Place
Utica, New York 13501-5618

DEDICATION

In memory of Mark, our youngest (25), whom we lost three years ago. When he was about six or seven I was writing a kind of fairy tale, "The Monarch," for my offspring. Mark was enthusiastic and kept me going with his periodic question, "Have you got another chapter done yet Dad?"

January 1990
Louis Mihalyi
Glenfield, NY 13343

Table of Contents

Railroad Gone	1
Bittersweet	5
Nuthatch	7
Striped Maple	9
A Lad And A Hoop	11
Weasel	14
Daddy Long Legs	17
Teasels	19
North Country Butterflies	21
Wild Calla	23
Snapping Turtle	25
Stinkhorn Mushroom	28
Moths	30
Horsehair Worms	32
Burdock	35
Tamarack	38
Bladderwort	40
Tree Swallow	42
Skipping Stones	45
May Flies	47
Little Brown Bat	50
Water Strider	53
The Fox Grape	55
Balsam Fir	57
Foxfire	59
Trout-Lilies	61
Nighthawk	63

Nasturtium	66
Whirligig Beetles	68
Chipmunk	70
Hazelnuts	73
Scouring Rush	76
Ticks	78
Mayflower	80
Song Sparrow	82
Eastern Worm Snake	84
Red-Tailed Hawk	86
Take A Lesson From Red Hen	89
Heron	91
Balsam	94
Hummingbird Moth	96
Slime Mold	98
Northern White Cedar	101
Parasol Mushroom	103
Flicker	105
That First Pocket Knife	108
Brown Creeper	110
Carpenter Bee	112
Giant Puffball	115
Engraver Beetle	117
Oak Rolltop More Than A Desk	120
House Wren	123
Sir Elk, the Penstand	125
Ape-Man Trolley	127
Mud Hen	130
Queen Anne's Lace	132
Bee Balm	134
'Blue-Eyed' Grass	136

CHAPTER 1

Railroad Gone
Not Forgotten!

The trains don't run through town anymore. Life, which centered around the arrival and departure of the daily trains, has shifted elsewhere. No longer can one thrill to the five o'clock (a.m.) flyer as it roared through town, its whistle on a continuous wail, some of its Pullman cars straight from New York. No longer do the small-fry count the cars as a lazy freight rumbled through the crossing.

The trains were dirty. If you lived on the leeward side of the tracks, you always tried to get your washing on and off the line between trains.

The trains were noisy. The early morning milk run kept the light sleeper awake as it stopped to pick up its load of milk from the milk station. Sometimes the delays at the crossing seemed interminable as the shifter moved back and forth sorting cars to leave on the siding. Sometimes the stationmaster would warn you that a hundred-car freight was coming so you could get on the other side of the tracks if you were in a hurry.

Trains Created Excitement

At one time when I was young there were four mail/passenger trains that went through town daily, two northbound and two south. This was in addition to the 5 a.m. and 11 p.m. flyers, the morning milk train and the almost daily freights. Four times daily a knot of observers would gather at the station. If school was not in session the knot would be swelled with a sprinkling of small-fry.

"Is she on time?" someone would ask Art Robinson, the stationmaster. "Yup. She'll be here in 10 minutes." Sometimes one of the more daring of the watchers would put his ear to the rail. Suddenly he would raise his head. "She's on her way. She just left the 'Falls,'" he would announce. With that announcement the small-fry contingent would back well away from the track and turn expectantly toward the south.

Before long we would hear the wail of the whistle as it neared the crossing a mile or so down the track. Then the louder blasts as it rounded the curve and approached our crossing. At last the locomotive would come screeching, hissing and belching into the station. The whistle gave its last screech as it reached the crossing. Clouds of steam spewed from the engine. Black clouds of thick smoke engulfed the station and sometimes sparks from the wheels of the cars added to the excitement as the train came to a halt.

Cars Hurriedly Unloaded

Art would have precisely positioned his mail cart alongside the track. The wide-opened doors of the mail car came to a halt beside the wagon. If express or other parcels were on the train, he would position his express wagon for the express car. The mail bags were expelled and the express unloaded with dispatch. Time was important. The train must not be delayed. Occasionally, when there was a large unloading to accomplish, some of the adults would give a hand.

All too soon the conductor would sound his "Board." The last passenger would scurry up the olive-painted steps. The conductor would heave his metal step on board and the engine would, with great labor, get the train under way. Sometimes the wheels would slip with a great crashing noise and exhalation of steam as the wheels spun momentarily on the track. The slow, measured chugging would gradually increase until it was a steady roar as the train disappeared out of sight down the track, thick black clouds of acrid smoke marking its way.

Coins Often Flattened

The show was over and the spectators gradually drifted away. If someone had placed a penny on the track the knot would scurry over to inspect the paper-thin disk of copper, all that remained of the United States coin.

It was a spectacular show, repeated four times daily, rain or shine, snow or hail. Sometimes a freight would be sidelined on the sidetrack to allow the mail train to pass. The brakeman would inspect the wheels for hot boxes. Rarely a box would need attention. With a hooked rod he would lift the door of the box, stir the oil soaked rags a bit and close the door. Sometimes one of the crew would take an enormous oil can and oil some parts of the locomotive. All of this under the watchful and curious eyes of a handful of potential railroad men.

Occasionally the railroad would put on a super spectacular show. Sometimes it was necessary to get a message to the engineer of an express-flyer as she roared through town. Art, holding a long cane rod with a broad loop in one end, would stand at the far end of the station. Attached with a spring clip was a message just received via the clicking telegraph. As the locomotive roared past, with the whistle at a constant wail, the engineer with a hooked arm would snare the loop, release the message and drop the cane hoop usually within a few yards. Art never had to go very far to retrieve his message stick for use another time.

Snow a Minor Inconvenience

Winter did not provide much of a problem. When excess snow fell, crews would be on hand to shovel around the station. Usually the "cowcatcher" on the front of the locomotive was all the plow that was necessary. But occasionally when large amounts of snow fell, a single locomotive pushing a massive plow would clear the tracks. It would roar down the track flinging the offensive snow many yards to the sides. Heavy snow might make an occasional train late. Only twice do I remember when heavy snows stopped the trains.

In the early days there was no high school in town. Nearby villages had high schools. To accommodate students the schedule would be adjusted or even a special train scheduled to take students to and from class.

If you needed to shop, the railroad took you to the nearby county seat or to larger cities farther away. The schedules were so good and reliable that Montgomery Ward was only three days away. An order mailed Monday morning was filled in Albany and returned on Wednesday afternoon. Occasionally special excursions were organized. It was possible on Sunday to go to the St. Lawrence River, take the boat excursion and return home that night.

Railroad Resurrection?

In its heyday the railroad was an important, integral part of our lives. It was our link with faraway places. It was an important communication and transportation system, it supplied us with necessities and the occasional luxury. To many it was a never-ending source of entertainment. To a considerable extent life in our little town revolved around the railroad.

But the railroad is gone. The tracks have been torn up. Only the embankments remain, a reminder of other days. The convenient automobile, along with radio and television, have laid it to rest.

In the north country it is nearly extinct.

I venture that as geologic oil becomes more rare, making the personal internal combustion engines most expensive, that there will be a resurrection.

I hope the resurrection will come in my time.

CHAPTER 2

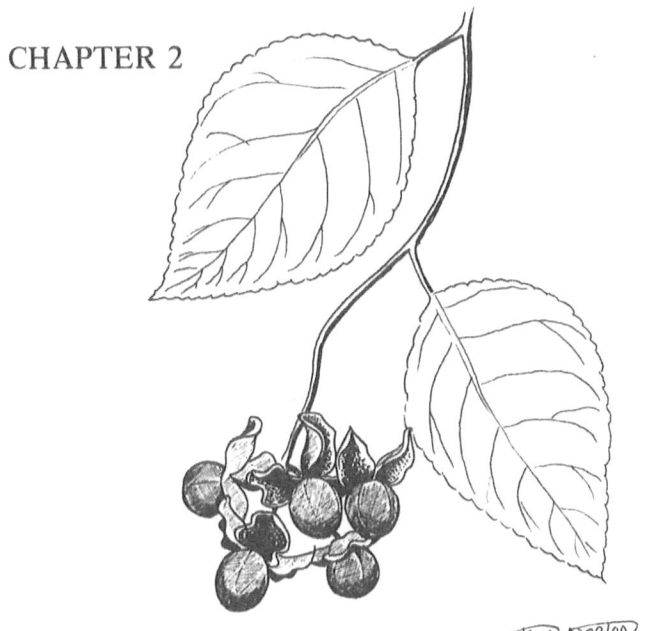

Bittersweet
Location Kept Secret

I first recall seeing the fruit of the Bittersweet at a tender age, while on a gathering trip with my mother. She knew of a patch and wanted some of the brilliant fruits for winter decorations. The scraggly vine grew over the limestone ledges not far from my home. We visited the spot on a warm Indian summer day one Fall.

It was one of those days that is etched permanently in one's memory. Frosts had done their duty and warned of the impending frigid storms of winter. Tender plants had folded their leaves for the last time. The chipmunks were busily gathering the last seeds to complete their winter larder. The maples were in full fall dress, yellow, orange and red. The ashes showed purple and lavender. The oaks were a brilliant bronze. It was a glorious day. I was just old enough to begin to appreciate the wonders of the various seasons.

My mother equipped me with a pair of small scissors and instructed me to carefully cut the cluster stem from the vine. She was concerned that the vine not be damaged. We also took sparingly of the fruit leaving clusters attached "for the birds and for new plants." I was fascinated by the orange capsules and enthralled later when they dried, split open and displayed the brilliant scarlet seeds within.

We returned with a nice bouquet to be met by a neighbor who insisted on knowing the location of our treasure. My mother reluctantly gave her the information.

A week or so later we happened to pass the spot to find that someone had picked all the remaining berries and in the process had torn many of the vines out by the roots. That taught me a lesson for I've since never divulged the location of Bittersweet to anyone.

The American Bittersweet (*Celastrus scandens*) ranges from Maine to Manitoba, south to Georgia and Mississippi. It is a vine running over the ground or low vegetation. When it climbs trees it may reach twenty feet in length. It has simple, oval, alternate leaves, two to four inches long and up to two inches in width. The greenish yellow flowers appear in June. These inconspicuous flowers are either pistillate (female) or staminate (male) but both appear on each plant. It is the berry-like, spectacular fruits that catch the eye. A series of dull orange capsules form in loose drooping clusters. These globular clusters when ripe split open to reveal brilliant fleshy coated scarlet seeds. The scarlet centers, framed by the orange scales dry easily and maintain their color for years. It is not surprising that such a brilliant product would attract the early herbalist. The berries were said to be good for stomach trouble and to alleviate the symptoms of tuberculosis. The steeped root was used by mothers in labor. It does seem to have some emetic properties and appears to increase perspiration. My own feelings are that because the berries were so spectacular it must have been thought that they had to have some medicinal value. Probably the greatest was the placebo effect.

The Bittersweet has many names as you might suspect: Climbing Bittersweet, Feaverwig, Feaverwitch, Climbing Staff Vine, Yellowroot, Climbing Orange Root. Years ago I heard an elderly lady call it Fall Orange Berry.

A number of years ago while duck hunting along the Black River I spied in the distance a huge orange stub. Close inspection showed it to be an ancient Elm trunk nearly covered with Bittersweet vines, with hundreds of orange fruits decorating the enormous trunk. It was like an immense fire-orange tower. I picked a quantity of the berries and showed my treasure when I returned home. A lady neighbor begged to visit the find. I declined to reveal its location explaining my reason. I offered her part of my gathering. She accepted the offering but was not mollified.

CHAPTER 3

Nuthatch
Difficult to Befriend

For many years I have been on intimate terms with chickadees. They come to my hand for sunflower seeds. They take seeds from my lips and from my chest when I am lying down studying the clouds. They follow me in little flocks as I walk around my woods waiting for me to stop and extend my hand. If I should hesitate they frequently will buzz my head to call attention to their needs.

These friendly little birds are easily tamed to come to your hand. After the first year of training the problem is solved. There always are a few older birds to set an example for each year's fledglings, who soon get accustomed to the feeding method and in subsequent years pass it off to their offspring.

But this is not so with the nuthatches. The red-breasted and white-breasted nuthatches are not so easily convinced. The nuthatches, together with an occasional brown creeper, join the chickadee flocks as they follow me. They feed close by and do not seem to be bothered by my presence. During these past years only very infrequently have I had a nuthatch come to my hand and these only were the red-breasted variety. I have stood many hours trying to convince them that my hand was as good a cafeteria as our feeding station but to little avail.

One day I had an idea, or rather I borrowed an idea. Some months earlier in one of his *Rural Living* columns, John Van De Water described how he used a scarecrow, which apparently closely resembled him, to get some beavers accustomed to the human form and thus allow John to make friends. It seemed well worth the try.

An old hunting coat was my starting point. It was so ragged, tattered and torn that my helpmate would not allow me to wear it. But it had comforted me on many a foray into the cold and I could never bring myself to discard it. This old friend I draped over a coat tree. A strip of wood, on which was fastened a flat scrap, projected out through a sleeve. This approximated my outstretched hand. A scrap of cloth stuffed with pine needles topped by an old cap completed the head.

Despite the weight of the heavy wool jacket and cement blocks on its base, my sculpture blew over shortly after it was first established. This led to tying it, using a hangman's knot, to a tree branch above, to keep it steady. A small can of sunflower seed on the outstretched "hand" completed the deception.

The chickadees found the seed within minutes. We watched for several days and soon discovered that a few nuthatches were finally taking seeds. After a few more days I stationed myself next to the dummy with seeds in my outstretched hand. It worked. Within a few minutes a red-breasted nuthatch lighted on the rim of the dummy's coffee can and, seeing the relatively open hand with its easily accessible seeds, immediately flew over. Within a half hour at least three different nuthatches made more trips to my hand than had occurred in all the preceeding years. Thus the scare (attract) crow worked. So, John, I owe you one.

CHAPTER 4

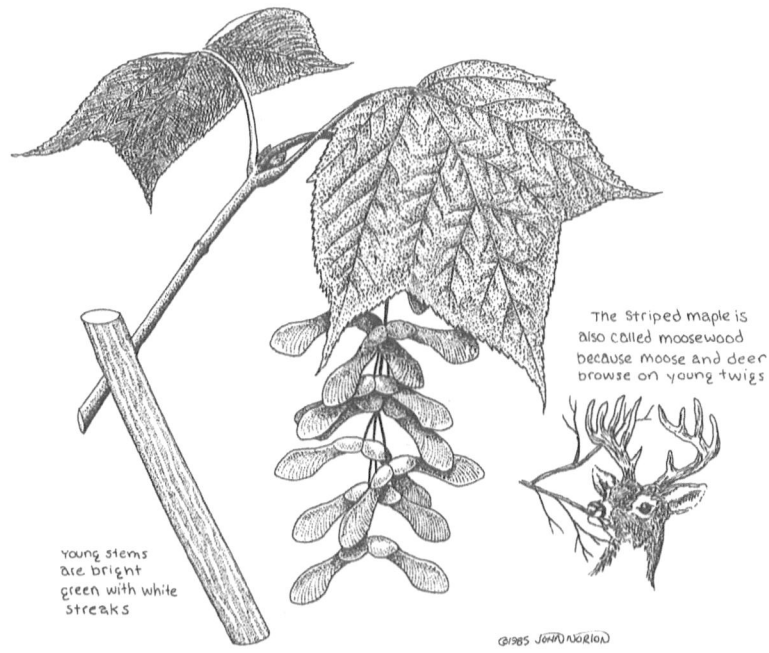

Striped Maple
Not Valued for Beauty

Of the dozen or so maples that one can find in the north country, the Striped Maple (*Acer pensylvanicum*), while quite common, is one of the lesser-known.

The woodland owner probably considers it a weed tree. Those concerned with the white-tailed deer consider it an important source of food in deer management. Rarely do I find anyone who considers it for its beauty.

Under ideal conditions it may reach a height of 30 feet with a trunk of perhaps 10 inches in diameter. I usually find it not more than 10 to 15 feet high. It cannot stand strong light nor can it thrive in deep shade so it is found in cutover areas and along the edges of woodlands. It prefers a cool, moist environment.

It is the bark of this tree that gives it its beauty. It is a smooth, semi-glossy olive in color with long longitudinal white stripes. With most trees, the young smooth bark gives way to a broken cork-like surface. The furrowed outer bark is dead and cracks as the tree increases in diameter. The bark of the striped maple, however, is alive. Thus, it continues to maintain its satiny-smooth texture. However, as it ages the bark begins to take on a swarthy, warty appearance. A clump of these striped stems is most attractive.

Another common name is Moosewood. This probably results from the fact that moose and deer relish the slender twigs, particularly during the winter months. In some areas that I visit the moosewood rarely gets over two or three feet in height because of the continual browsing of the resident deer.

The straight young twigs of this beautiful slender tree are red and green. It has very large paired leaves which have three lobes and resemble the foot of a goose, hence the common name goosefoot maple. In the fall these leaves turn yellow and red.

Both male and female flowers are produced on the same plant. The flowering takes place in May and June with pollination by insects. The resulting fruit, red in July, is the familiar two-winged maple samara. A recently cutover area will soon sprout a forest of striped maples. Within three or four years, some of these may be eight to ten feet tall.

When you put all of these attributes together, you come up with a very beautiful tree, a tree that deserves a much better reputation. It is another one of those beauties in nature that we have largely ignored.

CHAPTER 5

A Lad and A Hoop

The word "hoop" today means something entirely different, as a game, than it did when I started this business of living. Today, playing hoop involves two teams with one or more players on a side, a basketball and a hoop mounted on a pole with or without a backboard. In my early days it meant something quite removed.

In my early days, hoop referred to hoop rolling. The basic ingredients were a hoop and a stick. These were not purchased by doting parents, but were procured by the user. You found a barrel hoop or better yet, a tire rim, which was much more solid. Then with a strong stick, a foot or two long, you were in business. The hoop was started rolling and kept going by hitting it with the stick.

This technique was not instinctive. It required more than a little skill. A modification of the stick soon appeared that made things much easier. A nail was driven into an end of the stick at right angles to the long surface.

After the hoop was started rolling it was easily kept moving and guided by pushing it with the nail. Once in motion all you had to do was keep up with it. It was a simple pastime but rewarding. As one gradually gained skill the hoop could be kept going at the very slowest of speeds. It could be induced to take the sharpest of corners or make beautiful curves. At high speeds the skilled operator could make his hoop lay out almost flat when he took a corner.

You could always tell when there was a hoop roller in the vicinity by the constant sound of the nail scraping against the hoop as the driver urged his steed along. Did the operator tire of the constant screeching? Probably not. More likely it was a parent who had reached the end of his rope. In any event, a refinement appeared. A spool nailed to the stick provided a sort of bushing that rotated producing considerably less sound to say nothing of the lessened effort. Sometimes an operator would have a nail on one side of his stick and a spool on the other. This allowed for the best of both worlds.

Occasionally someone would acquire an iron tire from a wagon wheel. This might stand taller than its operator. The clever operator would easily run beside his steed pushing it from inside the front or use the traditional back and forth through the hoop, pushing and guiding it from either side. Sometimes a pair of skilled operators would perform interesting feats by driving a small hoop through a larger hoop as they both rolled down the street.

Every boy had his hoop. A good hoop would last a lifetime. Each of us treasured his vehicle. Maintenance was minimal. Basic maintenance consisted of replacing the nail as it gradually wore through. After a day's use my steel automobile tire rim was safely stowed in the woodshed to rest until the next session. Sometimes a gem, a special model, would be handed down from brother to brother. The steel models would be polished and usually attained a high sheen. Sometimes the driving stick would be decorated with designs of notches and spirals by a skilled carver. Most of us could recognize every hoop in town by sight as well as sound. Ownership rarely changed hands without permission.

It was a simple activity. It was a good activity that gave hours of rewarding pleasure. Probably the greatest benefit was the running that was required. We ran from morning to night. We did our physical training without complaint. We never suspected that we were partaking in an obnoxious activity, physical education, that in the future would acquire some ill repute.

One day, there appeared an embellishment. Someone came up with a way of adding to the noise. By carefully stomping with the heel on an empty evaporated milk can one could "shoe" himself.

The can was laid flat on the ground with the rounded side up. As one stomped on the round side the ends gradually curved over toward the center. With experience one learned just the right time to give the final stomp which clinched the edges on the heel of the shoe.

A few more stomps and the runner was solidly shod. With tin can shoes on each foot the runner now could clump audibly down the street behind his hoop. The rhythmic clump of the can shoes gave an added dimension to the hoopsters. It was a satisfying sound not unlike a horse trotting on a pavement. Now the scream of the nail on the hoop was augmented by the steady clump of the tin can shoes. There was one detriment to this fine addition. When it came time to become "deshod" the leather heel on one's shoe might be loosened. This did not endear the can shoe to the parents concerned.

Hoot Gibson and Tom Mix now charged down the street in pursuit of the iron ring. The good guys chased the bad guys. The black hats galloped frantically as the white hats gave chase. Occasionally a Knight of the Round Table would charge through town, his shining lance replaced by a gleaming curved hoop.

The equipment was simple. The game was free of complications, limited only by imagination and stamina. It appealed to a wide age range. It was simple enough so that the novice could take to the road without much training. There was room for developing skills. The skilled operators achieved status by displaying their proficiencies for the admiring novitiates. I wish I could invent a game with these characteristics. My financial status would be permanently secured.

Words mean different things to different generations. The hoop that my offspring play is entirely different from the hoop of my day. Both accomplish similar things, entertainment and exercise. Perhaps the current hoop is more sophisticated than the other. Certainly it is more costly.

CHAPTER 6

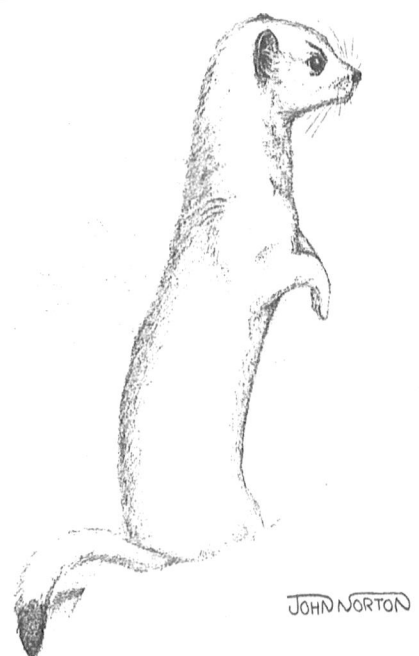

Weasel
Maintains Nature's Balance

We are all familiar with the term "Blood thirsty as a weasel." But few have seen this vicious bundle of fur. It was probably much more familiar to our grandparents and great grandparents than to the present generation. It is still around and doing well in its native haunts.

One day this fall toward the end of the hunting season I was standing on watch a day or two after a four-inch fall of snow. I was watching intently into the drive when out of the corner of my eye I saw some movement. I looked down to see a weasel scurrying along over the snow almost at my feet. It was hopping along poking its nose into every nook and cranny. A brief insertion was all that was necessary. Time for a single sniff and it was on its way.

It was headed generally away from me and was covering a swath about two feet wide. No lurking place for possible food escaped its nasal scrutiny. It was pure white with a black tip on its tail. After a few minutes it disappeared, blending into the snow. The last visible evidence was a black dot bouncing over the snow.

One evening just about dusk years earlier in a cold February my family was in a car moving slowly between two to three-feet high snow banks. We spied an ermine moving on top of the snow. We stopped the car and watched for better than five minutes as this animal scampered at eye level over a several square yard area. It went back and forth over the snow in systematic search. We surmised that there was some scent coming up through the snow. A fairly firm crust kept the animal from finding the hoard or from digging it up. It was a fascinating few minutes.

Kills With Abandon

Most predators kill what they need. But the weasel seems to kill with abandon, for the joy of it. When I was young my grandmother told me of a time when a weasel got into her chicken house. They ran to the house as soon as the attacking noise was heard but in the short interval before they arrived a dozen laying hens had been killed, neatly bitten behind the head. When I asked what she did she replied that they ate a lot of chicken during the next week or so and had relatively few eggs during the following winter.

There are species of weasels that range from the extreme northern tip of Greenland, south through Canada to the southern states and west to the Pacific coast. The genus name of these weasels, *Mustela*, is composed of two Latin words. Mus refers to "mouse" and Tollo means "to carry off." Thus the weasels are those who "carry off mice." All of the weasels that inhabit northern climates turn pure white during the winter except for a black tip of the tail.

There are several species that we might see in the North Country but probably the most common is the Ermine Weasel (*Mustela erminea*). This animal is slightly longer than a chipmunk but much slimmer. Its summer colors are brown above and on the side, white below with white feet. It is a carnivore, feeding on chipmunks, mice, shrews, birds, frogs, snakes and insects. It is one of our best mousers.

There is evidence that mating takes place in early summer. There is a short period of development of the eggs which then become quiescent for several months. Development resumes in late winter with four to nine young being born in mid-April. The total gestation period is from 205 to 340 days. This is incredibly long for such a small animal but the actual development time is much shorter. There seems to be evidence that the pairs remain paired throughout the year with the male helping with the feeding.

The weasel is hyperactive and hyperaggressive. It will attack prey many times its own size. It seldom walks but may take short hops. Its maximum weight is four ounces. It has a very high metabolic rate.

The weasel has scent glands and can discharge a foul musk when attacked. It does not spray as does the skunk. The musk is not used against other weasels. One trapping season many years ago we caught a weasel in one of our muskrat sets. It was late in the season and the fur was not prime but we decided for the experience to prepare the pelt anyway. We were aware of the scent glands but a slip of the knife as my brother was skinning it convinced us of the potency of this defense mechanism.

This animal has a valued place in nature. Were it not for weasels and other carnivores like the foxes, owls and skunks we would be overrun by mice. A balance must be maintained. The weasel is an important part of the other side of the scale.

CHAPTER 7

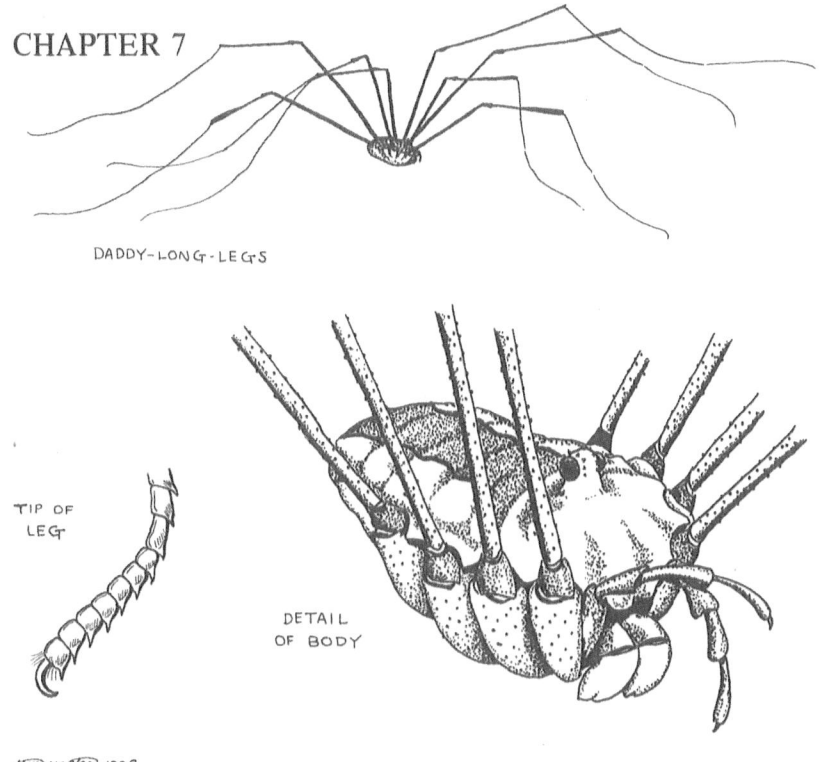

DADDY-LONG-LEGS

TIP OF LEG

DETAIL OF BODY

JOHN NORTON 1983

Daddy Long Legs
Animal Can Shed Its Limbs

Some years ago I had a rather striking bed of geraniums in a planter by my front door. A visiting friend recoiled in horror when she bent down to inspect the blossoms. "They're full of spiders," she almost shrieked. Actually there were a large number of Daddy-longlegs or Harvestmen resting on the geranium leaves. I did not try to correct her identification but rather tried to extol the value of these creatures.

I tried to point out that these long-legged animals are predators of small insect pests and thus are of value. The Harvestman is a great predator of mites and for that reason alone I consider him an asset. In addition to a variety of other insects it is said that the Harvestman feeds on snails and slugs, another plus if this is true.

Most people think that the Daddy-longlegs are spiders. And most people think that spiders are insects. Neither thought is cor-

17

rect. Insects have six legs and three body parts: the head, thorax and abdomen. Spiders have eight legs with the head and thorax sort of fused together. Thus their bodies have two major parts, the cephalothorax and the abdomen are merged into one. Its eight legs indicate that it is much more closely related to the spiders than to the insects.

The body of the Daddy-longlegs that I see is pea-sized. It is a kind of flattened oval. It hangs delicately suspended from the eight long legs which leave the body arching upward, then curving down and outward. In some species these legs may be thirty times as long as the body. I am intrigued by the coordination that this tiny body provides for these very long legs. To move, legs one and three on one side move forward with legs two and four on the other side. Then legs two and four on the first side move forward with legs one and three on the second side and so on. This alternation of legs and sides provides surprising agility.

Since each species has its predators the Daddy-longlegs is no exception. When in danger it can quickly shed one or more of its legs. Preoccupied with the writhing leg in its grasp the predator allows its prey to escape. There are many similar instances in nature when a part is sacrificed to protect the whole.

The female deposits her eggs in the soil, under bark on trees, or other secure places. She gives them little parental attention. This is unlike some of the true spiders which nurture their offspring to a considerable extent. The population of Harvestmen builds during the summer and is quite high as the end of the season approaches. This probably accounts for the name as they are most abundant during the harvest season.

The Daddy-longlegs is a harmless animal. He will not hurt you. In fact you may find him beneficial. Take some time and look closely at this creature. Look at the way the long legs carry him around, a method that has been much studied by space specialists. Look carefully for the periscope-like eye stalk which allows him a wide viewing range. You will be looking at a marvelous mechanism, obscure, seemingly insignificant but marvelous.

CHAPTER 8

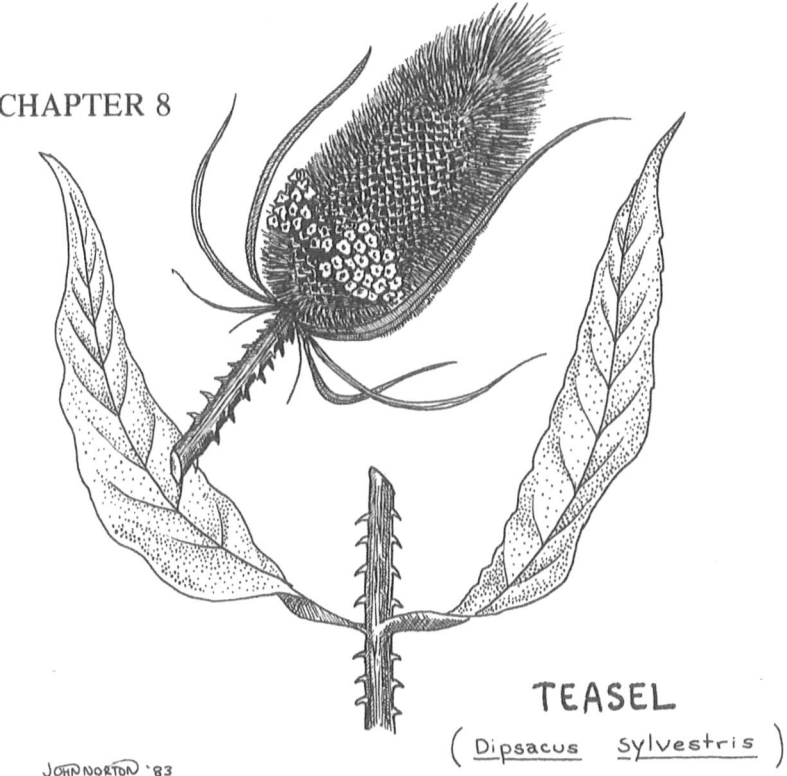

Teasels
Winter Sentinels

One time when I was quite young I was out driving with my mother. As we drove along the highway my mother spied some tall plants. "Remember this spot," she said. "Those are Teasels. We'll come back in the Fall and get some." In October we returned to the patch and I was introduced to the Teasel.

I was not impressed. She was interested in the fruiting head which she wished to dry to use in her dried flower arrangements. To me it was just a prickly dried weed. The central part of this fruiting head was a cylindrical affair with many hooked projections. It was a number of years before I began to appreciate the beauty of these flower heads. I guess that, as time passes, a certain amount of maturation occurs, in spite of ourselves.

The Teasel may grow up to ten feet in height. Those I see, growing in waste land and along the road side, rarely get above six feet. It is a biennial. The first year it forms an attractive ground-hugging rosette. The second year it comes into its own pushing up a stalk that dominates the immediate landscape.

The flower comes into bloom in late summer or early fall. The lavender to pink blossoms are quite large in keeping with the stature of the plant. These flowers may be six to seven inches in length. The leaves are long and narrow, paired, and embrace the stem. The Genus name, *Dipsacus*, is Greek for thirst. This refers to small pockets at the base of the stems that hold water.

There are several Teasels or teasel-like plants. I think the one that I see is *Dipsacus sylvestris*. The Teasels are aliens, imported from Europe. Its introduction was not accidental as was the case with many of our wild alien plants. It was deliberately introduced as it had some commercial value.

The dense head of the flower comes equipped with a large number of stiff hooks. It is these hooks and their cylindrical arrangment that gave it its use in industry. These "Teasels," as the flower heads were called, were used to card wool. They were also used in woolen factories to raise, "tease," the nap on the textiles produced. In earlier times most woolen factories had commercial plantings of teasels in their vicinity.

But times have changed. Different, better methods are now used in the textile industry. The plantations of Teasels are no more. What remains are descendants of those that escaped to the country side. A range map shows that they occupy a broad band from New England through the central part of the country to Colorado and Utah. Apparently they do not do well in the South or the North Central States.

As the times changed so did I. I now appreciate the beauty of this flower. I now can appreciate the grace of the dried flower head as it stands erect about the winter snows, etching the bleak winter landscape with its intricate design.

Some years ago while on a trip I stopped at a large garage for repairs. To pass the time I wandered around outside the building. In an open area at the rear was a large, luxuriant growth of Teasels. I picked several stems and took them in to the manager hoping to make some time-consuming small talk. "You've got a patch of teasels growing out back," I said. He looked at my offering. "Yeah," he said, "We're going to bulldoze that all over and make a parking lot." So much for auto repairs and small talk and Teasels.

CHAPTER 9

The Harvester

North Country Butterfly
An Aphid-Eating Villain

The image most of us have of the butterfly is that of a delicate, colorful, gentle insect. In its adult form, it feeds mostly on nectar from flowers or, in some cases, does not feed at all. The butterfly larval form feeds voraciously on specific plants and while this may cause some defoliating damage, we generally do not cast the butterfly in a vicious or villainous role.

Many insects feed on other insects. This may be during their early developmental stages or as adults or both. But butterflies do not fit into this role. Thus, it comes as a surprise if not a shock to find that there is in the north country a butterfly that is a vicious predator.

The harvester butterfly (*Feniseca tarquinius*) in its larval state feeds almost exclusively on aphids, the ubiquitous plant lice. It appears to prefer the plant lice that live on deciduous trees and shrubs, particularly those that infest the alders. Since the alders like damp areas, here is where you are most likely to find the harvester. Ash, witch hazel and beech also harbor aphids that the harvester likes.

Tarquinius is a small butterfly, probably not much more than an inch when its wings are spread wide. The wings are a brownish orange with irregular black borders and random black spots. It is not a spectacular specimen as butterflies go.

The harvester caterpillars are even more unspectacular. Small, greenish, with many long hairs at the joints, they blend in quite well in their aphis pastures. Here they feed voraciously on their woolly prey. In a 10-day period they go through only three molts before being ready to pupate. This unusually rapid larval development may be attributed to their high protein aphis diet. Other butterfly caterpillars, feeding exclusively on plants, require considerably longer periods and more molts to reach the pupal stage.

"What good is it?" is a question we usually ask when confronted with a new species. We think that everything has to benefit us directly to be good. If we see no benefit we are likely to classify it as bad or perhaps harmless. Most butterflies would probably be classified as good in that they contribute beauty to our environment and accomplish some pollination. True, some, like the white cabbage butterfly, can cause consternation in the cabbage patch. The harvester butterfly seems to enhance the butterfly image as a whole with its appetite for the "harmful" aphids. Since there is the possibility that we don't know everything, perhaps it would be good to abandon the need to classify everything according to character. We might even sleep better for it.

CHAPTER 10

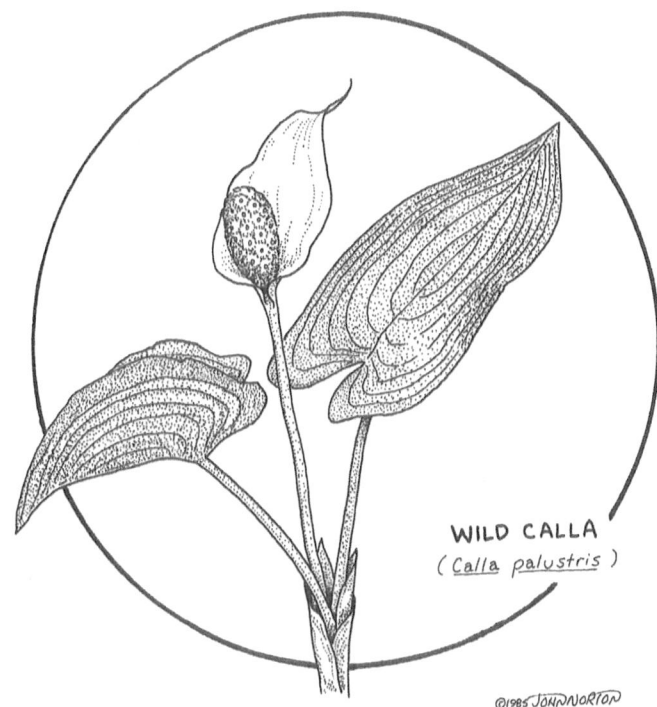

Wild Calla
Brings 'Tropical Look'

One pleasant June day I was looking through the tag alders that surround the small pond from which I draw water to irrigate my garden in dry weather. A brilliant, flashy patch of creamy white caught my eye. This had not been there several days earlier. I made my way to discover a rather spectacular flower, the Wild Calla (*Calla palustris*).

This member of the Arum family likes its feet wet. It goes by the names of Water-Arum and Bog Arum, indicating its preference for moisture. Actually, the flower of this swamp beauty is rather insignificant. It is its other peculiar arum parts that make it spectacular. The tiny, golden-yellow flowers are clustered on an elongated rod-shaped structure called a spadix. This is the "Jack" in the Jack-in-the-pulpit, which also belongs to the arum family. When covered with tiny yellow blossoms it is arresting. Highlighting and enhancing this golden spadix is a brilliant, white, leaf-like structure called a spath. This is the roof that covers Jack's pulpit. In the wild calla the spath does not curve up and over the spadix as it does with the Jack-in-the-pulpit. It partially curves around the spadix and then flattens out, providing a striking white frame for the yellow club-like spadix. The overall effect is delicate brilliance against the dark marshy background.

Visitors are surprised when I show them this showy structure. It looks so tropical that they have difficulty believing it to be native. The showy flower is long-lasting. But gradually its white fades. By the end of the summer the spadix becomes a cluster of bright red berries.

The wild calla is found from southern Canada to New Jersey and Pennsylvania, from New England west to Wisconsin and Minnesota. Depending on its location it blooms from May through August. The leaves are heart-shaped. The plant rarely grows over a foot in height and likes acid soils.

The wild calla should not be confused with the Calla lily whose species are native to warm Africa. These plants cannot survive our winters and must be dug up at the end of each summer and stored indoors. Their soil and water requirements are also considerably different.

I have never seen the wild calla in abundance. A friend once told me of a boggy area that was literally white with wild calla blossoms. I was never able to visit the area and have always felt somehow cheated that I missed this spectacular show. My wild callas are scattered here and there among a patch of tag alders that surround my pond. They bloom year after year. The only attention they get is from my gaze as I feast on them with my eyes.

CHAPTER 11

Snapping Turtle
'Ugly, Vicious'

One day during the summer I was twelve I was fishing on the Black River. I had acquired my first levelwind reel after months of saving. Reversing the butt of my trusty telescope rod I was fast becoming a devotee of the art of bait casting.

To reach an opening in the eel grass that might harbor a nice pickerel, I stepped out on to a small rock that was protruding from the water. The rock began to move out into the river. I was having my first and only snapping turtle ride.

This vicious reptile is widely spread from the Rockies to the East Coast and from Southern Canada to the Gulf, excepting southern Florida and southern Texas. I have found him in high Adirondacks and seen him in sluggish Oklahoma streams. For most he holds a fascination bordering on the horrible.

Because of his nature he doesn't need the full shell protection that most of our more retiring turtles require. The under shell or palstron is much restricted. The upper shell or carapace has three rough keels or ridges which reduce with age. He is drab,

25

black to brown in color on top, lighter below. Were it not for his great size and nasty nature, the snapping turtle (*Chelydra serpentina*) would be a relative unknown.

The snapping turtle matures when the carapace is about eight inches long. The mating season ranges from April to November and thus a very extended egg laying period exists. There is evidence that the female may produce more than one clutch of eggs during a single season after a single mating. Also, sperm may be stored by the female to fertilze eggs during a subsequent period. Females may mate with more than one male during a cycle.

Leathery Eggs

After a gestation period of from two to six weeks the eggs are laid. Digging with her hind legs the dedicated mother will deposit from twenty to thirty eggs. These nests can be placed almost anywhere but usually soft, easily worked sand is chosen. After the eggs are covered the female leaves. Having done her duty, her responsibilities are ended, her dedication gone.

The ping-pong ball-like, leathery shelled eggs remain in an incubation period of from 50 to 125 days depending on temperature and humidity. Eggs laid late in the season will hatch the following spring if they are below the frost line. Egg predation is high, raccoons, skunks, foxes and crows being the principal predators. After hatching, the young turtles are food for herons, bitterns, other turtles, and fish. The newly hatched snapper has a temper all his own. While he is small he must make his way to the protection of water rapidly. If detained he will not hesitate to snap at your finger. This little bite is relatively harmless but not so that of the adult.

It is the vicious, quick snap and the strong sharp jaws that give the snapper his reputation. You are well advised to avoid the business end. A large snapper could easily sever a finger. It could irreparably damage an arm. Despite this danger, or perhaps because of it, the snapper provides a fascination.

Serpentina is also tenacious with is grip. Once he has seized an object he is reluctant to let go. If it appears to struggle his jaws become immovable. Once while fishing with a friend we caught a large snapper. We induced it to bite the center of a sappling which we then laid across the sides of our boat. The turtle remained suspended in the boat for most of the day while we fished in relative safety.

The snapper has another reputation that is much less known. He is good eating. The flesh is light and sweet. In some areas of the country the snapping turtle meat is a highly regarded delicacy. Mostly thought of as scavengers, they are predators catching their own living food and also herbivors eating some plant life.

During the winter the snappers hibernate. By November most are buried in the mud, their life processes slowed for a long winter of inactivity. Sometimes they will move around. One time during my high school days, I watched a large snapper through the ice. I had fallen on clear ice while skating on a small creek that flowed into the Black River. It was a bright day in January. The reptile moved ever so slowly from one mud bedroom to another. Perhaps the bright sunlight had awakened him or perhaps it was the shock wave from my fall.

If you must pick up a snapper, grab both hind legs with the back of the turtle away from you. This will point the business end of the turtle away from your body and reduce the likelihood of a chunk being missing from your knee. The tail is a handy grasping handle but should be avoided as the weight of the animal (which can reach thirty pounds or better) pulling down can cause injury to its backbone. When it is first picked up the animal may emit a scent which is not very agreeable.

Ugly, vicious, mean-tempered, not something with which you would want your daughter to associate, nevertheless this creature is an integral part of the scheme of things. All things fit. Every living thing has its place. In that respect we are all alike. You and I, the elm tree, the snapping turtle, the tree swallow and the porcupine are all part of nature's plan.

CHAPTER 12

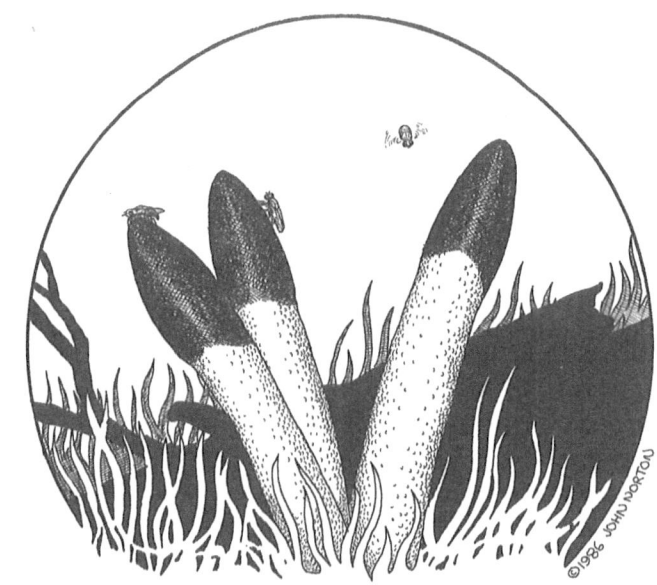

Dog Stinkhorn
Mutinus caninus

Stinkhorn Mushroom
Just Sits and Stinks

There are a number of stinkhorn mushrooms. They are aptly named.

I think the stinkhorn I see is *Mutinus caninus*. It looks something like a single cow horn and it has a powerfully offensive, fetid odor. It rarely reaches six inches in height. Those I have seen were at most 3 to 4 inches tall. "Well," you say, "if this is such a nondescript, insignificant thing why waste space on it?"

It may be insignificant to us. It may appear to have little value and less appreciable effect on our lives but it exists and therefore is important. Perhaps it is just as important in the overall scheme of things as you and I.

Perhaps we may be more important in that we have the capacity to destroy our environment while the stinkhorn mushroom just sits there and stinks. Perhaps there is not so much difference after all.

It first appears as a pencil-like cylinder, seemingly sprouting from a tiny egg. The slim, conical tip elongates and becomes pink. The cylindrical stalk is hollow. The glistening pink tip, covered with a gelatinous material, gradually turns from pink to tan and then brown. Within a day or two this fruiting body has withered away. The cycle has been completed and awaits another turn.

Why does it have this repelling scent? What is repulsive to some may be attractive to others.

I have noticed when the tip has turned brown that flies congregate and crawl over it. Perhaps this is a means of distributing stinkhorn spores. The scent attracts the flies that pick up the spores from the sticky gelatinous tip. The flies then leave the spores at some distance as they fly away.

Fortunately, probably because of its size, it does not produce an abundance of its odoriferous signature. You have to get down close to it to savor its rank scent.

Also it is not common. I see one or two each year in my woods. Thus its fragrance is never a problem.

The fungi, of which the mushrooms are a large part, come in many forms. The stinkhorn is an unusual form. To the eye, uncolored; by the nose, it is simple and beautiful. Nature is replete with beauty. Sometimes it is necessary to make an effort to see this beauty.

CHAPTER 13

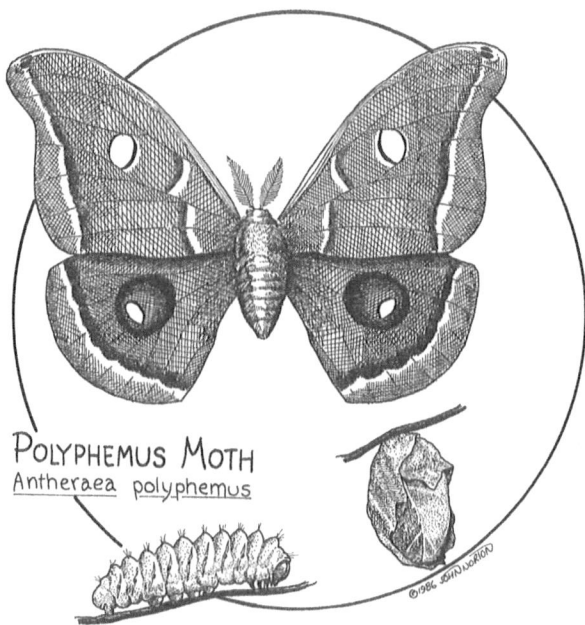

Moths
Antennae Are Vital Organs

Moths, as opposed to butterflies, are largely nocturnal. That is, most moths are active during the hours of darkness. The most easily observed distinguishing characteristic of moths, when compared to butterflies, is their antennae. This also has to do with their nocturnal activity.

Scent seems to be the most important sense for these night fliers, particularly when searching for a mate. The antennae are their organs of smell.

Thus the antennae of most male moths are large and feathery, while the butterfly antennae are plain extensions, some with a sort of knob at their ends. The feathery construction provides enormous surface area to capture and detect molecules of female scent.

Experiments with marked male moths have shown they can detect and find a female that is over a mile away. Released downwind, the male can home in on the female, relying on the difference in numbers of scent molecules that fall on each antenna. When one antenna is removed the male can detect the female but cannot determine her direction.

Since moths are nocturnal their coloration is less brilliant than butterflies. Nevertheless, some moths are quite colorful and with respect to size, spectacular. One of these, one of the giant silkworm moths that inhabits our area, is the polyphemus moth, *Antheraea polyphemus*. This beauty has a wing-spread of up to six inches. Its cocoon is made of a fine, strong silk, hence its classification as a silkworm moth.

The wings of the moth are of various shades of buff, olive to a greyish brown. The forewing features a clear yellow-bordered eyespot. The hind wing has a black border and a prominent dark eyespot. The adult polyphemus never feeds. Its larval form, which easily reaches three inches in length feeds voraciously on the leaves of the maple, oak, birch and other deciduous trees.

The three-inch caterpillar is spectacular. A rich green, it sports a red head and red spiracles along its sides. Along the back are a series of reddish protuberances. Some yellow lines decorate the sides. The chunky body is conspicuous with its segmentation.

One evening when I was young we watched moths gather around our porch light which my mother had left on for that purpose. Suddenly a large tan moth appeared, to be followed shortly by several distinctly larger buff-colored moths. I watched, fascinated, as my mother explained what was going on. She had several polyphemus specimens in her collection and so the process was not disrupted.

While polyphemus is not abundant, it is common wherever deciduous food is plentiful. I rarely see it as my woods are largely conifers. If you are near a hardwood grove the chances are good that polyphemus is there.

CHAPTER 14

HORSE HAIR WORMS
(class GORDIOIDEA)

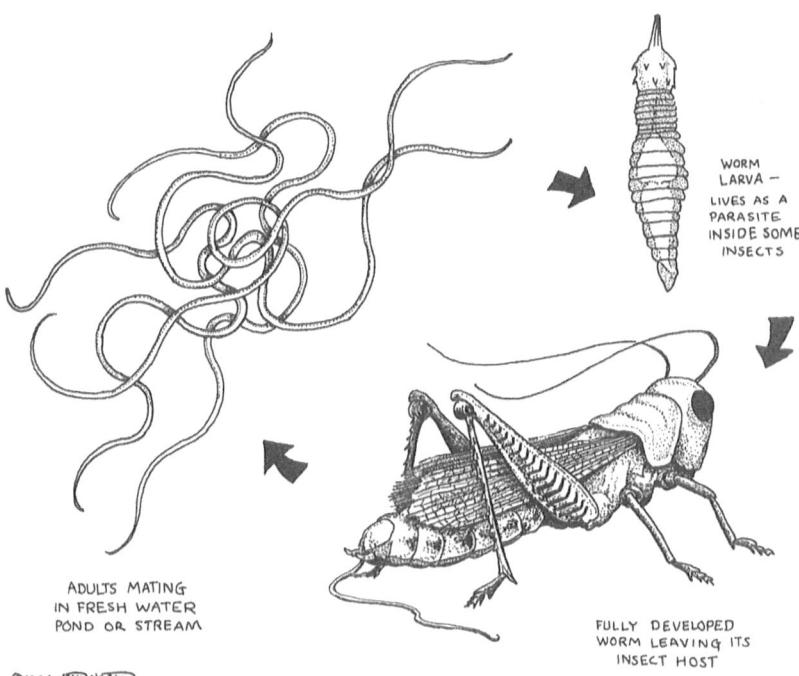

ADULTS MATING IN FRESH WATER POND OR STREAM

WORM LARVA — LIVES AS A PARASITE INSIDE SOME INSECTS

FULLY DEVELOPED WORM LEAVING ITS INSECT HOST

©1984 JOHN NORTON

Horsehair Worms
A Youthful Encounter

It was just about dusk. I was established on the bank of the Black River with a cane pole and my trusty casting rod. I was probably in my twelfth year. The bullheads were biting and I was going to catch my share. I had baited up. My cane pole was secured out over the water by two crotches, one inverted in the mud to hold the butt down. Its baited hook was out a few feet from shore. My casting rod was propped against my tackle box, its enticing hors d'oeuvres well out in the river. This arrangement enabled me, so I thought, to cover a maximum of river bottom.

I was at a favorite spot. The air was warm. My shirt collar and sleeves were buttoned down against the onslaught of the mosquitoes. My hands and face covered with copious layers of "Lollicapop," that old time odorous insect repellent. Lollicapop's effectiveness depended less on its scent capabilities than on its thick applications. But its scent was not all that bad. I still have a nearly empty tin which I take out once in a while to savor the now magical and nostalgic aroma.

Watching for Nibbles

While watching my poles for the telltale nibbles I watched the reflection of the clouds on the surface of the water in the gathering darkness. Out of the corner of my eye, in the shallow water at my feet, I noticed a slight movement. As I focused on the movement, a thin wavy line appeared to move slowly through the water. An empty tin can was at hand. I quickly used it to scoop up the wavy line. And that is what it was, a living, writhing, wriggling, wavy line. In the dim light it seemed to have a front end but I could see no recognizable head.

I lighted my kerosene lantern but could make neither head nor tail of the beast. The fish started biting so I placed the can in a safe place to carry home and devoted myself to the business at hand. A thunder storm came up. I sat huddled under a piece of old canvas shielding my lantern, bait pail, fishpail, tacklebox and the tin can with my animated wavy line. The fish bit well. By the time the thunder had faded away I had my fishpail half full and was headed for home.

The Mystery Worm

The next morning I showed my mystery to my mother who said she thought it was a hairworm. There was nothing about hairworms in the books we had at home. Inquiry about town provided no additional information. After a day or two I released my prize and then waited several years before acquiring more information.

What I had been looking at was one of the horsehair worms. There are about two hundred thirty species of these worms which belong to the class *Nematomorpha*. The largest are over five feet in length with a maximum diameter of about one quarter inch. They range in color from a faint clear yellowish to a dark brown.

The life cycle is quite interesting. The male deposits a drop of sperm at the genital opening of the female. After a period of time the sperm activate and move into the genital pore. The female shortly begins a period of egg-laying that may last several weeks. She may deposit in the neighborhood of four million eggs. These eggs hatch within a month and start looking for a host.

Aquatic Insect Nursery

Some find a nursery within the bodies of aquatic insects. Many use terrestrial insects as hosts. *Gordius aquaticus*, probably the species that I saw, forms a cyst on grass blades. As water levels lower the grass is eaten by grasshoppers, beetles, crickets and other land insects. Once inside the obliging host the cyst breaks down releasing the larva which then grows to many times the length of its host. The skin of this animal is only one cell thick. This enables it to absorb its nutrient requirements from the host along its entire body length without undertaking any digestion whatsoever.

It appears that the host, by this time sick and dying, has a need for water. It seeks out the nearest pond, puddle or stream and succumbs to its disease. The now adult horsehair worm emerges to start the cycle all over again. It has no means of feeding and subsists on stored nutrients until its reproductive activities are completed.

A Seething Mass

A few years ago I was exploring a ditch that always had a small amount of water. I came upon a small, shallow pool that seemed alive. It was alive with hundreds of horsehair worms churning in a seething mass. These worms were each about a foot long. They formed an almost solid ball about a foot in diameter. They were a mud brown in color, very much like the mud bottom over which they cavorted. Had they not been in such motion they would have been invisible against the pool bottom. I assumed I was witnessing a reproductive ballet, the last act in this particular life cycle and left them undisturbed.

While the horsehair worm is parasitic, it is of no danger to man. You need not be wary of it. In fact since it has some potential in controlling some insect pests, you might regard it in a favorable light. It has its part as do you in this grand scheme of nature.

CHAPTER 15

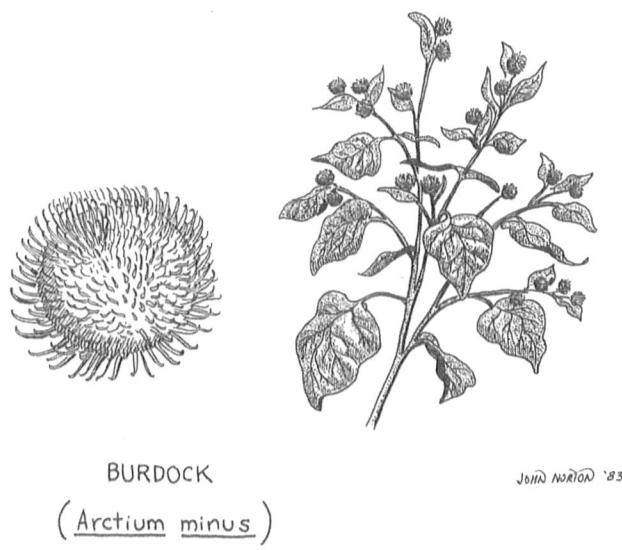

BURDOCK

(*Arctium minus*)

JOHN NORTON '83

Burdock
A Much Maligned Plant

The common Burdock, *Arctium minus*, is the bane of the mothers of small boys and the owners of long-haired dogs. This alien weed is thought to have come from Europe very early with the colonists or, as one author suggests, perhaps it came even earlier with the Vikings. In any event, this problem plant came early to our shores and established itself quickly and permanently.

It is a biannual developing an extremely long tap root that allows it to survive under the most extreme circumstances. It is well established throughout the United States with the exception of the southwest and a small area around Lake Superior. The blossom is an attractive pink-purple. A well established burdock in full bloom is a beautiful sight. These blossoms, framed by the large broad leaves, are not very much appreciated.

From these attractive blossoms develops the bur fruit. The flower is surrounded by many hooked bracts which eventually harden to form the hooks that make up the bur. Inside the ripened fruit one may find up to twenty-five elongated seeds. The burdock reproduces only from these seeds.

When I was small, probably seven or eight, we used to gather these burs in late summer before they were ripe. The hooks were sufficiently sturdy to perform their function. Packing a handful of burs into a ball about the size of a tennis ball, we played a game of tag. The person who was "it" would attempt to "tag" the other players by throwing the bur ball. There was no question when a tag was made as the missile would stick fast. This was especially true if it lodged in one's hair.

When the "hair tag" occurred the game would be temporarily halted while the projectile was disentangled from the hair. Once retrieved the game would continue. Sometimes we could not free the ball and the sad individual would have to go home for maternal help. This course brought down the wrath of those dear creatures who had nurtured the players. Eventually a decree went out and the games were halted. The burdock thus passed out of our lives.

The bur with its cache of seed is an ideal method of seed dispersal. The numerous hooks attached themselves to any passing animal frequently to be deposited considerable distances from the producing plant. I once found an old fox den that was surrounded with a healthy tangle of burdock plants. The nearest patch of burdocks that I could remember was a half-mile away. I assumed that the fox occupants picking up burs during their foraging, had bitten them out of their fur on arrival at the den. The seeds thus inadvertently planted had established a fine stand around the fox homestead.

Once quite popular, the burdock is not much used currently for medicinal purposes. Leaves, flowers, seeds and roots were used in various ways. Herbals list a great variety of ailments that called for the use of burdock preparations. Apparently the root was favored. It seems that at one time in some areas the plant was cultivated. I have read several times that when under cultivation a ton of roots could be expected per acre.

The leaves and stems are bitter. As a result grazing animals avoid the plant. There are not many insects that feed on the burdock.

Thus, its long tap root and general hardiness make for permanence once it becomes established. Birds feed on its seeds, which is a plus in its favor. Pheasants, in particular, feed on the seeds which stand well above the winter's snow. It provides shelter for birds and small animals. Try penetrating a well established burdock jungle. The previous year's stalks with their dried burs, the sturdy current year's growth with its green burs will soon convince you of the safety of its shelter.

An alien, maligned by most, its beauty ignored by many, the burdock has adapted well to its new land. Perhaps, as one friend said, it has adapted the land to itself. Nevertheless, it is a part of the grand scheme. Perhaps some day we will discover, despite its irksome fruit, that it has some fine value which at present we are unable to fathom.

CHAPTER 16

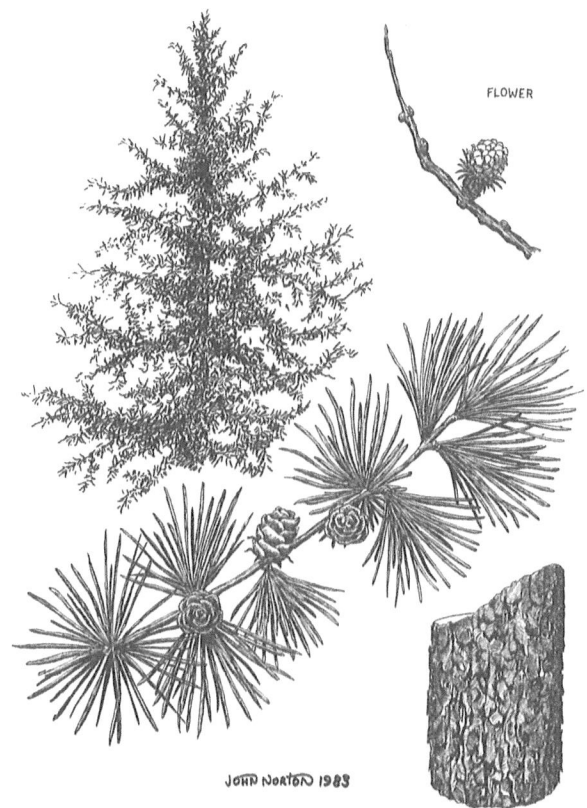

Tamarack
A Special 'Evergreen'

The term "evergreen" usually conjures up a tree whose leaves are needle-shaped and which keeps its needles for one or more years. But not all evergreens are trees. Not all evergreens have needle-shaped leaves and not all needle trees keep their leaves for more than one season.

The American Larch (*Larix latricina*) is one of these renegades. It is a beautiful, tall, conical tree that each spring puts out an abundance of soft short needles which are shed the following fall. In full bloom the tamarack is a sight to see. Each spring as the tree takes on its delicate blue-green clothes it also adorns itself with a myriad of beautiful rose to grape juice colored blossoms.

The soft needles are only about an inch in length. On the previous season's growth they appear singly. But on older growth they appear in clusters of ten or more. In cross section they are awl-shaped or triangular. In the fall the blue-green needles turn to a yellow before being shed.

The rose-colored female blossom eventually produces a small, three-quarter inch cone that may persist for several years although most are dropped during the second year. From these cones tiny winged seeds are released to the whims of the wind.

Somehow I prefer tamarack to the name larch. I suspect it is because I first learned to call it tamarack after having been read some Indian lore that involved the tree that shed its needles. I can still see, in my mind's eye, a birch bark canoe silently gliding along a sluggish stream. It slips past a huge tamarack, the regal guardian of the dark, damp, misty swamp. I remember little more of the story. But tamarack sticks in my mind.

The tamarack is largely confined to the Lake States, New England and thence north across Canada to Alaska and up to the Arctic Circle. It is a tree of cold swamps reaching a height of 80 feet and a diameter of up to two feet. Its wood is hard, heavy, coarse-grained and light brown in color. It is very durable in that it resists the processes of decay. Thus it finds uses as utility poles, fence posts and the like.

I once visited a gentleman who showed me a picnic table by a lakeshore in front of his cottage. He claimed that it had been constructed from a tamarack felled on his property thirty years before. For thirty years it had withstood the onslaught of weather and decay. It still looked sound to me as though it had another thirty years of service to give.

It became necessary several years ago to cut a large tamarack on my property. I cut the trunk into several large pieces which I flattened on one side and placed in convenient spots around my woods as benches. They persisted for a number of years in good condition. They did not last for thirty years but longer than other similar benches of other wood species.

I do not know whether there is any special meaning for the word tamarack, Indian or otherwise. But for me tamarack is special. For me the tamarack is another of the many examples of the great diversity, the great beauty in nature.

CHAPTER 17

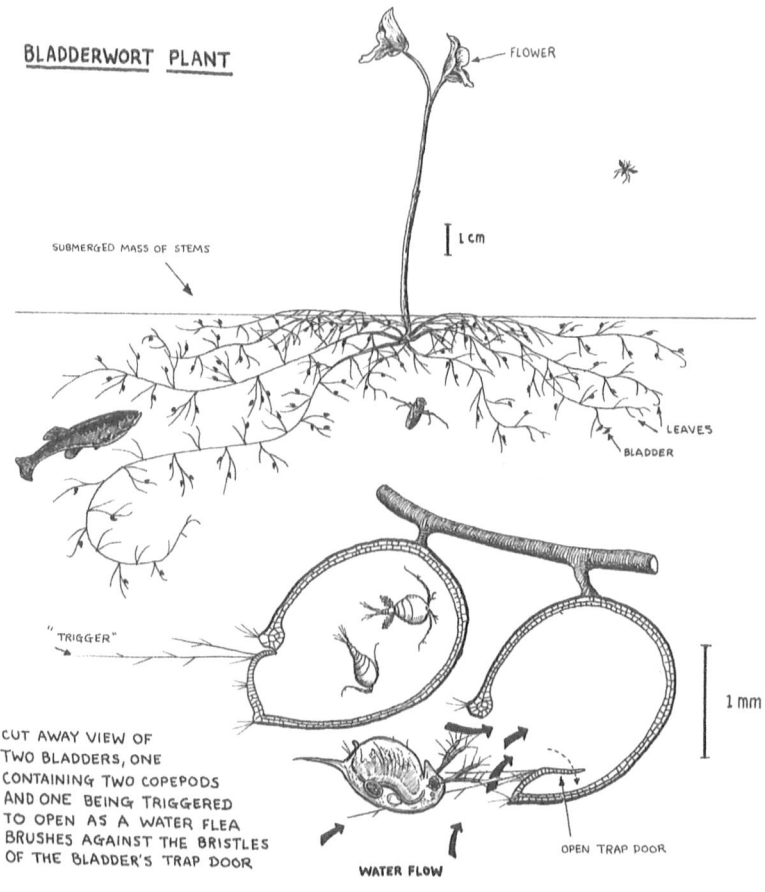

CUT AWAY VIEW OF TWO BLADDERS, ONE CONTAINING TWO COPEPODS AND ONE BEING TRIGGERED TO OPEN AS A WATER FLEA BRUSHES AGAINST THE BRISTLES OF THE BLADDER'S TRAP DOOR

Bladderwort
Seen But Not Recognized

A most interesting aquatic plant, that probably many have seen but not recognized, is the bladderwort.

This is a delicate, tender plant with horizontal underwater stems from which submerged forked filamentous leaves are produced. From these stems flower stalks project well above the water surface. At the tip of these stalks appears a delicate flower that reminds one of the snapdragon. The color, depending on the species, ranges from yellow through purplish to white.

The flower stems may rise to two feet above the water surface.

The seeds produced winter over for next year's cycle. There also is a vegetative form of reproduction involving the production of winter buds which survive the cold dormant season. Where abundant, the bladderworts are an important food source for marsh feeding birds, moose and deer.

What makes this plant interesting and unique are the bladders, from which it gets its name, that are scattered along the submerged stems. These tiny bladders are animal traps. They are so designed as to capture small aquatic animals and protozoa. These bladders are urn-shaped with a lid over the opening. When prey is in the vicinty of the opening the lid snaps inward creating negative pressure which sweeps the tiny prey inside. The lid then closes and the deed is done. The swimming life is trapped inside. Apparently the stimulus for triggering the mechanism is not well-known.

Some years ago I was casting for bass on the Black River, I was on the inside of a bend where the water was quite shallow. A cast a little too far toward shore landed my lure in a bunch of green weeds. I reeled in a large mass of a delicate plant which I had not seen before. The many tiny bladders attached to the stem were very visible. I knew then what I had and placed the plant in a pail of water.

Later at home I looked at the little bladders under some magnification. Many were like small aquariums with little life forms, mostly protozoa, swimming around inside. Some were empty. In some the prey appeared to have disintegrated. It appeared as though the bladder had begun to digest its catch.

According to one source there are perhaps a dozen species of bladderwort in the northeastern part of the country (75 or so worldwide). I believe the one that I see most frequently is the greater or common bladderwort (*Utricularia vulgaris*). This has many bladders scattered among the filmy leaves and has underwater stems up to three feet long.

These fresh water plants will be found in quiet, usually stagnant water. A muddy bottom with decaying vegetation is ideal. This is because of the many tiny animal forms that feed on the decaying vegetation and its companion bacteria. I do not find the bladderwort to be abundant. But I manage to see a specimen or two each year. One time I happened on a small pond that was loaded with floating bunches of this bladderwort. Look closely the next time you find a delicate filmy water weed. It may be a bladderwort. If so you will be holding some intense drama in your hands.

CHAPTER 18

Tree Swallow
Carefree Flyer

I spent many happy hours as a small boy lying on my back on the lawn watching the tree swallows. Their graceful aerial maneuverings kept me occupied by the hour. I still find pleasure, during odd moments, watching these carefree flyers. When no one is around I'm apt to again lie back on the lawn and return to those carefree days.

The tree swallow is the first, of the several swallows that move up the Atlantic coast, to arrive in the spring. I used to be very puzzled about their early feeding habits. It seemed to me that they always arrived well before an ample supply of insects was available. They always seem to be first found over open water where some water insects are present. But I used to wonder how they were able to find enough insect food for sustenance.

One day I read the sleek, diminutive tree swallow (*Iridoprocne bicolor*) was the only swallow to eat appreciable vegetable matter. Studies have shown that some twenty percent of their diet may consist of berries and seeds. This explains how they can exist early in the spring well before insect hatches occur. It also explains the several times I have seen rows of feeding tree swallows on the shore ice of my marsh. They were feeding on seeds that had been frozen in the ice.

Before the colonists arrived the tree swallow nested in holes and cavities in trees, stumps and the like. With the advent of bird houses this swallow quickly adapted itself to a new abode. I usually have one or two nesting pairs about my yard. They do not seem to be choosey about the type of dwelling I supply. Their main requirement seems to be that it be in the open and not surrounded by vegetation. Bird boxes placed in or at the edge of my woods are never used and rarely investigated. Those on single posts or on the trunks of isolated trees are in demand.

There always seems to be conflict. Tree swallows do not nest in colonies. So there is competition and quarreling between nesting pairs. Eventually they select dwellings that are well spaced and peace returns. If I have been lucky enough to have a bluebird favor me the tree swallows soon drive him away. But in turn the wrens evict the tree swallows. At last some sort of truce is reached with the wrens filling up the remaining unoccupied houses with twigs so as to discourage any further nesters.

The male tree swallow, about six inches in length, sports steely greenish-blue upper parts with pure white under parts, thus giving it the names of blue-backed swallow or white-bellied swallow. The female is about the same size and has similar coloration, often more dull. She is the nest builder producing up to six eggs when things are ready. Feathers, particularly white feathers, are a desired nesting material. When I clean out my nest boxes I always find feathers woven into the nest.

If I have them, I usually put out a supply of feathers when I see the birds investigating my apartments. I think it sometimes influences them to make a selection from among my offerings. Sometimes they will play games with my feathers before consigning them to household furnishings. A feather will be lifted high above the ground and allowed to float down. They seem to pick those that are the best floaters. They will swoop in and around the drifting feather, occasionally catching and lifting it back up. Rarely do they ever let it touch the ground. Finally after having thoroughly tested its aerodynamic qualities the feather will be taken to the bird house.

The first to arrive, they are the last to leave. Although they may disappear from your garden and lawn you will find them congregated near open water long after the other swallows have left for Central and South America. Many tree swallows winter in the United States, some as far north as Long Island. This may be the reason they are first on the scene in the spring.

Iridoprocne is a friendly and interesting bird that should be welcome anywhere. He eats tremendous numbers of insects. The hordes of mosquitoes that he consumes should delight any homeowner. I am certain that when he uses my yard as his summer address my outdoor comfort is increased. I enjoy his chatter as he gleans the mosquitoes and other insect pests from around my home. I take pleasure in his aerobatics.

CHAPTER 19

Skipping Stones
Each Generation's Mystery

Almost every boy has tried it. Not many have had the opportunity, the water and the ammunition, to perfect it. To me the art of skipping stones is a never-ending source of simple, self-fulfilling pleasure. I have to admit that in recent years my forays into the stone skipping competition have been minimal.

It all started many years ago on a Sunday school picnic. The location was a stream that had negotiated the ravines and gulfs of Tug Hill to flatten out on one of the limestone terraces not far from town.

Cascading over the upper layers of Tug Hill sandstone during the preceding millenia, the stream had carved and then honed myriads of flat, round stones with soft rounded edges. The stream was lined with fascinating stones from coin size to small pie plates.

When near water and a supply of stones a series of irresistible forces causes any small boy to attempt to "fill the pond" with the stones. Witness the toddler, still learning the coordination of walking, who, if left to his own devices near a stream or pond, will drop into the water whatever is handy.

We examined the collection of stones at our feet. The persistent stream had polished the stones to a smooth, silky finish. It was a pleasure just to hold them. A friend threw one into the stream. It hit the water and bounced to the farther shore. We experimented. The stream was not very wide. Every stone easily skipped to the opposite bank.

A short distance upstream the water flattened out and ran relatively straight for several hundred feet. This gave us a long stretch of water. We wondered how far we could skip a stone. The possibility of skipping more than once did not occur to us.

But with the first stone the game changed. The first stone skipped several times. Now the object was to see who could skip a stone the most times. We honed and sharpened our technique and soon were skipping stones almost the entire length of our flat run. Our supply of desirable stones began to diminish. We were skipping our stones upstream.

Partly because a new supply of stones had to be found and partly to test a theory that skipping stones downstream would give us more skips and distance, we moved to the upstream end of the flat. The new supply of stones was good, but strangely our distance did not seem to increase nor did the number of skips. In fact, we seemed to think that our performance was better on the whole when skipping upstream.

Some time ago an article appeared in the *Smithsonian* which pointed out some of the problems involved in studying and understanding the mechanics and physics of stone skipping. While the author felt that given the impetus (mainly money) the mysteries of stone skipping could be explained. He also opted for leaving the phenomenon alone.

I fully agree. Rather than reduce stone skipping to a set of equations, why not let each boy, whether 6 or 60, discover the phenomenon for himself. Let each individual determine the proper way to curl the finger around its edge. Let him, through trial and error, discover the best angle for the stone to hit the water, and then the angle to make the skips execute a curve. Each generation should be allowed the experience, the excitement, and then the pride in mastering the art of stone skipping by itself.

CHAPTER 20

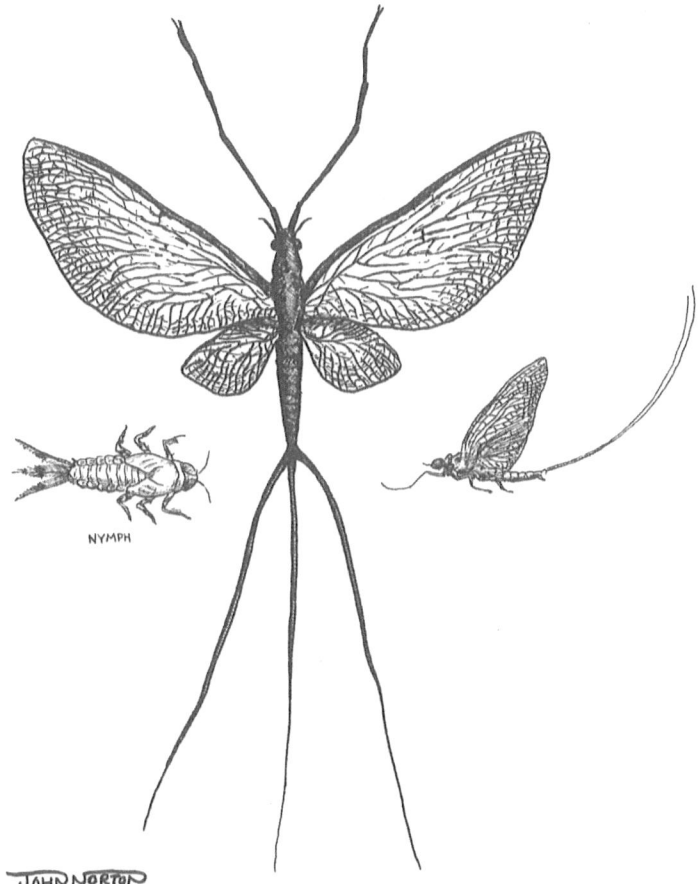

May Flies
Nature and Its Names

There seems to be a general rule about the names of things in nature. It says that the more widely known a plant or animal is the more names it has. The May fly is no exception. It is known as the eel fly, shad fly, willow fly, cisco fly, trout fly and on and on. On the American side of Lake Erie, May flies are called Canadian soldiers. On the Canadian side they are called American soldiers. The May fly is the only insect that has two adult molts. In Europe even these molt forms have names.

The May flies belong to the order *Ephemeroptera*, so named

because of the brief ephemeral quality of their adult lives. Worldwide there are about 1,500 species. In North America we have well over 500 species. The May fly is a soft-bodied insect characterized by a tail consisting of two or three long filaments. Another characteristic is the upright stance of the wings when at rest.

May flies are aquatic and strictly fresh water. They inhabit the most placid of ponds and the swiftest of streams. They have many modes of feeding and obtaining oxygen.

The nymph stage may last from a month to six years, all of this in water or mud. When it comes time for molting the act is accomplished in seconds. From then on the lifetime is limited. The adults eat nothing after this molt. Their mouth parts and stomachs have degenerated. They cannot harm you. They are destined to die within hours or at most a few days.

When the adult transformation comes it comes with a rush. In the swift Niagara river at the brink of the falls the nymphs shed their skins. Millions of adults arise from the torrent as it plunges over the brink. Swallows dart into the mist to feed at the bountiful table.

At almost any time during the summer you may see a cloud of dancing May flies. A few hundred to a few million males will gather to rise and fall in an undulation in a typical nuptual dance. Sometimes the undulations are almost hypnotic. Each species seems to have its particular dance step. Females moving into the cloud will be seized by males to fly off to complete the mating process. The final act is the deposition of the eggs in water, each species doing this in its own individual manner.

The numbers that are involved in this life cycle boggle the mind. At every stage millions are lost. Predators of the May fly are legion. Birds, fish and other insects dine on the May fly at every opportunity. Climate, and environmental changes account for the loss of countless millions. Yet each year, except where pollution has taken its toll, the May fly hatch renews at its former magnitude.

A number of years ago I was on a field trip. We had left Central New York by bus and were going along Onondaga Lake when we ran into a blizzard of May flies. Visibility dropped to zero. Flies were smashed against the windshield. The driver attempted to clear his vision with the windshield wipers. This made the mess worse. Windshield washers helped to spread the mixture evenly. The bus came to a halt. After a few minutes a breeze cleared the air. The driver scraped a hole for vision and proceeded to a nearby town and its gas station to wash his windshield down.

The cloud of insects was well up in the air. It was so dense as to darken the sun. When the driver came back inside the bus he brought hundreds of May flies clinging to his clothing.

One May evening while fishing for bullheads on the Black River I built a small fire to aid the lighting task of my lantern. An after-dark hatch of May flies began to dance in the lights of my lantern and fire. Every so often one would dip too near the flames and disappear with a light snap. As the tempo of the hatch increased so did the tempo of the snaps. Soon there was a continual hiss as hundreds of May flies met their doom. I finally quenched the flames disturbed by the carnage I was causing.

This fantastic, delicate animal, essentially defenseless, maintains its numbers by an incredible over-production. It is kept in bounds by its many predators some of whom might not live were it not for the bounteous feasts. The intricate network, the interrelationship of living things in the food web is well illustrated by the May fly cycle. I am awed by nature's ways. I am humbled by the intricate, the complicated machinery that we call life.

CHAPTER 21

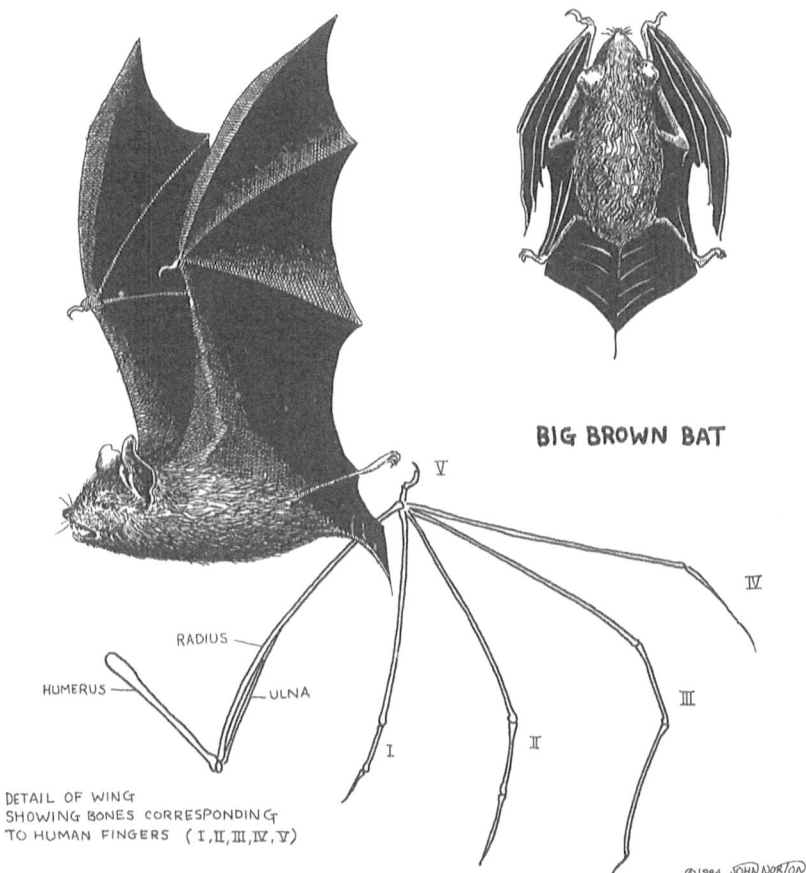

Little Brown Bat
Valuable Insectivore

There are a half dozen or more bat species that are common in the north country. One of the bats most of us in the north country are likely to see is the little brown bat (*Myotis licifugus*).

This marvelous little bit of aeronautical engineering is only about three to four inches in length with a full wing spread rarely exceeding 11 inches. Its rich brown back gives it its name. The wings are delicate membranes which are supported by four greatly elongated fingers. The thumb of this flying hand is a kind of claw-like appendage that it uses to crawl around on vertical surfaces. Its average weight is four to five grams which may nearly double in the fall just before hibernation.

It is insectivorous but does not catch its prey by mouth. Most are caught in the folds of the tail and wing membranes. If the prey is small it may be removed and consumed in flight. Larger insects are taken to some resting place for leisurely consumption.

The eyes are small, hidden and used largely to distinguish light from dark. It is the auditory apparatus that is spectacular. The ears are very large and so designed as to pick up echoes of supersonic frequencies that are emitted through the nostrils. This echolocation or sonar is fantastic in its sensitivity. Experiments have shown that bats can distinguish and thus avoid vertical wires only 0.12 millimeters in diameter. Pulses of sound pour out through the nostrils, hitting various objects in the flight path and are reflected back to be picked up by the large sensitive ears. These reflections are interpreted, evaluated and in that sense the bat "sees" in the dark.

Water is obtained by swooping over a pond for a drink. Mating takes place in the fall before hibernation. A delayed fertilization takes place in late winter. There also may be spring matings with immediate fertilization. Only one offspring is produced after a gestation period of 50 to 60 days. The young appear from June on through the summer. Being true mammals each youngster is nursed for three to four weeks at which time it takes to wing and thereafter provides its own food.

By late October the little brown bat begins its hibernation. This is a true hibernation. The body temperature drops to just above the freezing temperature or perhaps occasionally slightly below. The breathing rate drops from well above 100 breaths per minute to less than ten. The heart rate which normally may be in the neighborhood of 250 beats per minute is reduced to 175 or less. The animal is conserving fuel for the long cold winter ahead.

We tend to think of bats as hibernating in caves but for some species, in the absence of this preferred winter abode, a hollow tree, your attic, an undisturbed woodpile, may just be suitable.

Some years ago a student, after cleaning out the family woodshed in February, brought me a tiny bundle of fur. I was apprehensive that having broken its dormancy I might not be able to feed it and it would die. I had a supply of meal worms and tempted it with a succulent wiggling morsel as it lay on the bottom of its cage. The sharp teeth flashed and I could hear the "crunch, crunch" as the hors d'oeuvre disappeared. I felt assured that I could keep it alive until spring.

Each day I placed as many meal worms in its cage as it would consume. After the second day it would be found each morning hanging from the top of the cage. It began to recognize its feeding time though it was during the afternoon. When I opened the cage door to place the dish of meal worms on the floor it would immediately move down to break its fast. I was aware that its water requirements were met by taking drinks on the wing from ponds. The size of the cage prevented any flying and swooping but I placed a container of water in the cage and refilled it each day with clean water. I had to assume that it was adequate. I never saw the bat take a drink but it appeared healthy when I released it at the end of March.

I once found the mummified body of a small bat caught in a bundle of last years burdocks. Apparently it flew too close and entangled itself on the burdock hooks. The hot weather dehydrated and mummified the little body.

Bats evoke an unwarranted fear in many people. While the fear is unjustified it is nevertheless real. Groundless fear and superstition lead many to eliminate bats whenever they appear. Because of this and the destruction of their roosting, nesting and hibernating places, many of our bats are becoming endangered.

There is a general rule with respect to mammalian reproduction that says the smaller the animal the higher its reproduction rate. The elephant has a long gestation period and a long nurturing period. Elephants do not reproduce very fast. Mice and other small rodents have fantastic reproductive rates, under ideal conditions producing several litters each year. Bats are an exception on this rule. Generally speaking, each breeding female produces only one offspring each year. This reduced reproductive rate does not allow rapid recovery when bat populations are hit with catastrophe. There are some bat species that do produce more than one offspring at a time.

The little brown bat we live with is harmless. It is a valuable insectivore. Many hundreds of insect pests are destroyed each night by each bat. Bat houses, which are usually open at the bottom can be constructed to encourage bat residency. I am sure that the bats around my home contribute greatly to my outdoor comfort. They are the only effective nocturnal predators of mosquitoes. I do what I can to encourage their residency.

CHAPTER 22

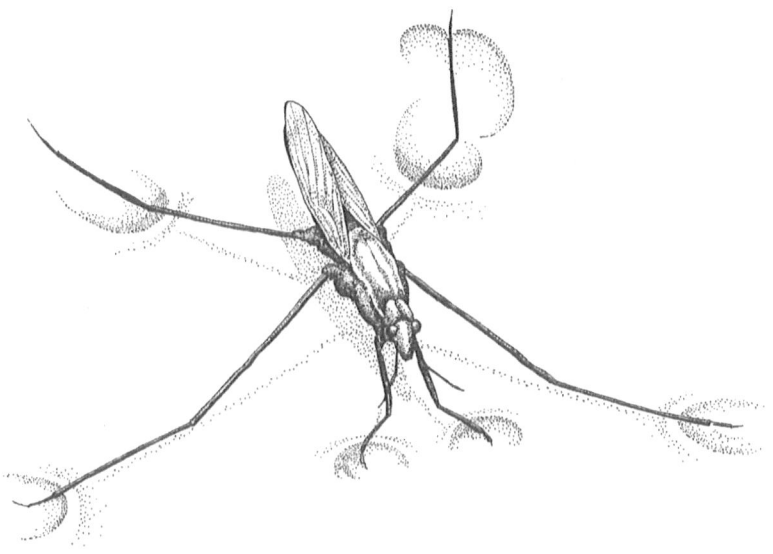

THE WATER STRIDER

©1984 JOHN NORTON

Water Strider
Unique Locomotion

One of the first water insects to appear in the spring and one of the last to remain active in the fall is the water strider or skipper. This insect takes our fancy when we are young. The fascination of being able to skate on water holds our attention for a few years gradually dissipating until we give it a casual glance as it skims across the surface of a quiet pool.

But this insect merits a little more attention. It takes advantage of a peculiar quality of water that produces an incredibly tough skin. The water strider lives in an environment that consists of a smooth, hard surface. On this vast shimmering plane the water strider lives, forages, reproduces and carries on all the basic life activities that are necessary to maintain the cycle.

The water molecule is a polar molecule. That is, it has a strong positive charge on one side of the molecule and directly opposite there is a strong negative charge. The molecule of most substances are such that the electrical charges are arranged in a symmetrical manner with little or no polarity.

If you remember your general science, unlike charges attract and like charges repel. Thus, in a body of water the positive poles of each molecule repel the positive poles of other water molecules but find a strong attraction to the negative poles. In the center of this body of water the repelling and attracting of billions and billions of molecules on any given molecule produces a balanced effect and it is as though there were no forces acting on this molecule at all.

But at the surface of the water all of the forces are lateral or downward or inward. There are no molecules above the surface to pull upward. Thus those molecules at the surface have a net inward force and are bound tightly together to form a very tough strong skin. For the amount of matter involved this film is incredibly strong.

This is called surface tension. It is the property that allows the porous weave of a tent fabric to shed water but allows air to pass freely. It is the property that makes the washing of clothes difficult unless the surface tension is broken by some chemical, a detergent. This is the property that the water strider uses to move with such speed and agility in its environment.

If you have ever floated a needle on the surface of a cup of water you know about surface tension. The water strider also knows about surface tension. A true six-legged insect, the water strider has modified its legs for this glassy environment. The fore pair are used for grasping its food. The middle and rear pair rest on the surface and provide the drive for this skater.

There are about 20 species in North America. One species is marine and may be found far out at sea. Some species have wings. Some species can dive and remain under water for long periods (several hours). Some species will quickly drown if submerged.

The water strider, sometimes called the Jesus bug, is a scavenger. It feeds on other dead or dying insects that fall to the water's surface. Eggs are laid from early spring through the summer. Attached to solid objects near the surface, they hatch within about 14 days. The young are very similar to the adults and are immediately as active. The adults winter in crevices, or under sticks and stones. With the first appearance of clear water in the spring they also appear.

In nature, every niche, every slot has its complement of living things. The water strider successfully occupies a habitat that on first glance might seem to be formidable and undesirable. Yet, through its adaptive qualities nature stocks all of its cubbyholes.

CHAPTER 23

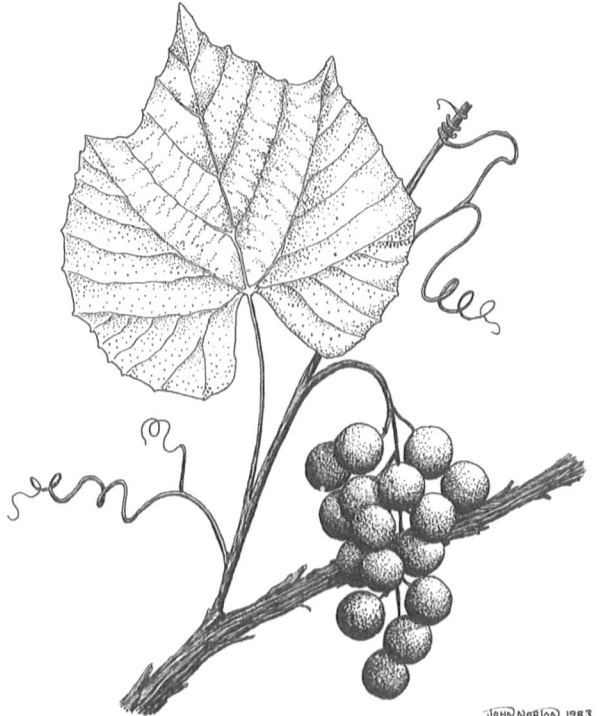

The Fox Grape
Purple Stains of Fall

One of the many good things about the Fall months is the profusion of wild produce that becomes available for the gathering. Among the many nuts, fruits and berries that are available during the late summer and fall is the fruit of the wild grape. Some kind of wild grape is found almost anywhere in the United States and Canada.

When the Vikings made their voyages along the Eastern coast of North America they found the grape in abundance and gave it the name of Vineland. I think that the grape I find most common in my travels is the Fox Grape. This grape produces nice clusters of fruit which can easily be snipped off with a pair of scissors. I usually get around to the grape harvest after we have had several frosts. The frosts have depleted the annoying insects making my forays into the field a pleasure.

I slip my belt through the bail of a small pail. My container thus hangs from my belt leaving both hands free for the harvest. One hand holds the grape bunch. The other snips it off and it is deposited quickly into the pail. To do the job efficiently you do not need to discriminate. Pick everything within reach. If there are green grapes on the bunch do not worry. They seem to add something to the flavor of the final product. If it is late in the season and the bunches are dried, harvest them just the same. The essentials of the juice are still there merely waiting for your technology.

There are several places that I visit where the vines have climbed well up into the trees. Here a ladder is a necessity. Sometimes I find the floor under these trees littered with fallen bunches. I harvest these with no hesitation. If I have been lucky and the season has been good my return home is accompanied by several baskets of the purple fruit.

My hands will be stained purple. My shirt front and my pants where I have wiped my hands will also be adorned. If I have hit the vines at the right time my stomach will be filled necessitating little or no supper that night.

Gathering the harvest and getting it home is perhaps the easiest part of the operation. Now comes a series of inspections and washings to insure as pure a product as possible. Strip the grapes from the stems, being sure to remove any decayed fruit. Place the grapes in a large kettle, crush and add enough water to barely cover. Cover and bring to a boil, then simmer for about ten minutes. Place in a jelly bag and suspend over a bowl until the dripping stops. A much clearer jelly with result if the bag is not squeezed. Follow the directions for any grape jelly found on pectin packages or in cook books. If it is grape juice you want, add sugar to taste. Fill jars and process in boiling water bath for 20 mintues at 180 degrees F.

It gives me great pleasure when I view the shelves in my cellar loaded with rows of jelly jars of purple grape jelly and the fat mason jars holding their royal grape juice ambrosia. The winter months ahead will be all the sweeter.

CHAPTER 24

Balsam Fir
An Evergreen Treasure

I would guess that the Balsam Fir is one of the most popular, if not the most popular, trees in the North. Certainly it is the most popular of the evergreens.

This popularity is largely due, I believe, to the delicious aroma of its pitch or resin. This scent is not only delightful but it persists. The balsam Christmas tree gives weeks of wonderful odor to the home. The needles of the balsam tend to remain on the tree longer than do those of the spruces.

When I was young our Christmas tree always was a balsam. The perfume of balsam pervaded our home during the weeks around Christmas. Today, the scent of balsam immediately brings back the warm glow of those early days.

There are about nine species of true firs in North America of which the balsam is probably the most widespread. It occupies a wide belt across our Northeastern states and much of Canada. As the name implies, the needles of the balsam fir are soft and furry to touch. Spruce needles are apt to be very prickly. The cones on the spruces and pines hang down. On the balsam they are held upright like tiny candles.

The young bark of the balsam is covered with little blisters containing the aromatic resin. This resin, called Canada balsam, is used as a cement for mounting microscope specimens. The balsam will grow up to sixty feet and a large tree may have a diameter of two feet. Its principal use is for pulp with some minor uses as lumber.

Abies balsamea likes moist soil. It can be found in abundance in cold Northern swamps. It will, however, grow well on other sites. It makes a fine landscaping tree and graces many lawns. When grown in the open it matures into a stately conical shape.

Years ago every vacationer in the northern mountains brought home a balsam pillow. Local entrepreneurs would gather balsam boughs and painstakingly strip off the needles to stuff into the pillows. This was quite a task. Many boughs had to be relieved of their needles to fill one pillow. I tried it one time and soon tired of the tedious task. The purchasers would take home a lasting scent memory of days spent in the mountains.

We had a pillow when I was young that was filled with balsam needles in the early twenties. I still have the pillow which still exudes its fragrance. It is not as strong as in earlier years, but one cannot fault 60 years of mountain scent.

CHAPTER 25

Foxfire
Capable of Giving a Good Scare

It was during one of my first camping trips. I was around ten years old. The night was dark. I was returning to my tent through a marshy area. As I rounded a turn in the trail, I suddenly saw what appeared to be a corpse laying face down just to the side of the trail. It glowed with a soft, cold, dim light. Its arms were grotesquely angled upward. Its legs seemed to be half buried in the soft sphagnum moss.

I can still remember the chill that swept over me as I viewed the body. The "hackles" on the back of my neck rose as never before or since. My skin prickled all over. At first I could not seem to breathe. Then my gasps came so fast that a conflict developed between the incoming and outgoing air. My heart sent Richter scale waves roaring through my body. I was instantaneously drenched in copious amounts of sweat. My legs were lead and then rubber. Facing south I somehow managed to resist the temptation to set a new sprint record north.

Gradually the tempest in my body subsided into a mild typhoon. The body lying on the moss seemed really dead as it made no movement. I inched forward and with fantastic courage touched one of the outstretched arms. It was damp. It was spongy. It was stringy. There was no resemblance to skin. Almost immediately, in the dim light, the corpse became a tree trunk with a couple of extending branches. There was not the slightest resemblance to a dead body.

I broke a small piece off one arm and brought it up to my eye. It gave off a soft ghostly glow. By holding it near my arm, it shed enough light to allow me to see the scratches from the afternoon's blackberrying. I had captured some foxfire. Its eerie, slightly-green glow became a curious delight.

This luminescence occurs when certain very specific conditions exist. In a constantly damp, but not drenching wet, environment, a fungus starts to grow on dead organic matter. When the fungus has spread through its medium and conditions are right it begins to glow. Sometimes it appears to be confined to the outer surface. In this case the inner rotted shreds of wood glowed as vigorously as the outside.

Unfortunately as my specimen began to dry out it also lost its luminescence. The next day when I showed the log to my camping comrades, I was greeted with some skepticism and had to wait some hours for nightfall before vindicating myself. At the time none of us knew about the phenomenon. But all did agree that it was scary.

There are many examples of bioluminescence in nature. The common firefly is an example familiar to most of us. This cold, energy efficient, light fascinates scientists, intrigues the layman, delights the young. The diversity of life that surrounds us is astonishing. To be aware of even a small portion of this diversity evokes wonderment, respect, even reverence.

CHAPTER 26

TROUT LILY
Erythronium americanum

Trout-Lilies
A Blush of Yellow

I first knew it as the Dogtooth Violet or Dog's Tooth Violet. It is also known as Adder's-tongue. I was never very happy with these rather grotesque names for such an attractive little spring beauty and so when I first heard it called the Trout-lily I latched onto that name as being far more appropriate.

It is a member of the lily family. I associate it with many of my first trout fishing expeditions. So, for me, Trout-lily fits. Another quite acceptable name is Fawn Lily.

This early spring bloomer is found up to elevations of around 2,500 feet. It reproduces vegetatively from corms deep in the soil as well as from seeds. The corms have a "dog-toothed" shape. That and the violet-like shape of the blossom may account for that common name. I am at a loss as to a reason for its being called Adder's-tongue.

The Trout-lily (*Erythronium americanum*) appears in April

and May. It has usually completed its blooming cycle and its leaves are withering by the time the hardwood leaves are well developed. It likes moist woodlands. From its deep bed, down eight to twelve inches, the corm pushes a smooth stem upward through the soil. Two slender, oblong, pointed leaves unfold near the soil surface. These are a pale green, mottled with a lavender or purple and sometimes a little white. The stem continues up six to nine inches producing a single, beautiful, relatively large, pale yellow blossom. This lily-like bloom may be also mottled with purplish streaks.

The blossom has three petals and three sepals, six stamens and a pale green pistil. The net result is a delicate bell-shaped flower. On dark days and at night the blossom droops. The fruit contains many cresent-shaped seeds. It takes six to seven years after seeds are planted for blooms to be produced. During its first two to three years only one leaf is produced.

Several times a week we take afternoon or evening walks that lead us along a backwoods gravel road. One section through a beech-maple woods is carpeted with trout-lilies in late April. They all seem to come into bloom at about the same time. One day as we round a bend we will see a yellow blush on the ground, our trout-lilies sending greetings.

In my woods under some tall pines whose first branches are high above the ground is a spread of these fine flowers. These usually come into bloom a week or so later than those in the open hardwoods.

If it grew you can bet that our ancestors tried it out for medicinal purposes. And so it was with the Trout-lily. An herbal compilation that I consulted states that the *Erythronium americanum*, the Trout-lily, has emetic properties. It is used in poultices to reduce swelling and is supposed to be useful in curing hiccoughs. I find it useful in curing depression.

As far as I can ascertain the trout-lily is not an endangered species. However, I would suggest that we treat all wild flowers as endangered.

Look, savor, enjoy, but don't pick or dig.

The blooms are far more attractive in their natural setting than on your mantel. If you must grow them do not take your corms from the wild. Many flower-growing companies now have stocks of nursery grown wildflowers. Buy your corms from them.

We have a great heritage in the "wild." We should do everything we can to preserve it.

CHAPTER 27

Nighthawk
An Urban Dweller

The Nighthawk belongs to the group of birds called goatsuckers. This family also includes the Whip-poor-will. The term goatsucker comes from the ancient belief that these birds with their huge mouths sucked milk from goats in the fields. The Nighthawk is additionally maligned since it is in no way a hawk. It does not have the needle-sharp talons of a hawk. It does not have the curved, sharp hooked bill of a bird of prey. It is strictly an insectivore catching almost all of its food on the wing.

While this bird is not rare, it is a bird that the urban resident is more apt to see than is the rural resident. In days past the Mosquito Hawk, a name that is common in some areas, nested primarily in open gravelly areas, fields or on open rocks. It is now common on gravel roof tops in cities and towns. The gravel roof top provides an ideal nest setting. It approximates its naturally desired nesting choice and is nearly devoid of predators. The egg eating snakes, raccoons and other enemies do not normally frequent apartment or office roof tops.

I have spent many pleasant hours in the cool of the evening after a hot day watching the flight acrobatics of these fine flyers. About 10 inches long, it is much larger than any of the swallows that swoop after insects. *Chrodeiles minor* prefers dusk for his active hours. He usually flies high in the air straining the upper air layers of their insect populations.

He flies high and fast. He circles, hovers and dives. It is the dives that are most spectacular. Having attained sufficient altitude he launches himself almost straight downward. The bent wings are nearly folded as he streamlines himself. Just when it seems that he is about to dash himself against the ground or a building he gracefully executes an arc and climbs back to the heights.

Frequently at the end of these dives a booming sound is produced. This booming may continue all through the courtship and nesting periods. In some parts of the South the Nighthawk is called the "Bullbat," probably because of this booming sound and its dusk flying preferences.

The nest is no nest at all. It is merely a location. I once watched a female on the gravel roof of a school as she incubated her clutch. Two greyish white spotted eggs had been deposited on the gravel. There was no depression, no rearranging of the small stones. A spot was chosen and the eggs laid. During the day the female patiently covered her eggs, not so much to keep them warm as to keep them from getting too hot in the sun on the roof.

Apparently she only left the nest at dusk to feed. The eggs were laid early in June and in about three weeks, just before the school year ended, they had hatched.

From above this slim-winged bird appears to be sooty black. But rarely do we see him from above. From below he appears grey with a bright white patch on each wing. There is also a white band in the tail and white on the throat. His wings are long for his body length and when folded at rest they reach the end of the tail. When this bird perches on a tree limb it usually sits lengthwise along the limb rather than crosswise as with most other birds. The Nighthawk's cry leaves something to be desired. It is a raucous screech, a grating, rasping sound that belies the grace of this bird.

I do not see the Nighthawk as much as I did in the past. At one time he was the "in residence" mosquito catcher in almost every town. Visit any community at dusk and you would hear if not see the bullbat, particularly if the town had buildings with gravel or at least flat roofs. This does not seem to be the case any more. A recent announcement by the New York State Department of Environmental Conservation lists the Common Nighthawk under "special concern" meaning that it is not yet endangered or threatened but that there is concern for its continued welfare.

The Nighthawk has taken to city life with gusto. He has adapted to urbanization. He gleans the air of its mosquitoes and thus more than earns his keep. He is a bird that you should get to know and enjoy.

CHAPTER 28

Nasturtium
An 'Old Fashioned' Plant

My grandmother always had a bed of Nasturtiums. I remember standing in front of her bed, a carpet of rich verdant growth through which myriads of flowers poked their heads. She was very careful to pick each blossom as it faded. Not letting the flowers go to seed kept the bed blooming she advised. I was allowed to help her with this chore and so came to appreciate the spicy aspect of the nasturtium.

Whenever she fixed a salad and whenever nasturtiums were available, she always went out just before putting the salad together and picked a few nasturtium leaves and blossoms. These were folded in with the other salad ingredients to give her salads a distinctive flavor. She also always made her own dressings and mayonnaise. One dressing with a mustard base I remember with relish. This together with nasturtium spice gave her salads a distinction that would have put Betty Crocker or Ann Page to shame had there ever been a competition.

It was not until long after these tender years that I became aware of other varieties of the nasturtium. My grandmother always planted a low bushy variety. So I was surprised when I found a climbing variety and then a tall variety. My catalogs now make available several choices as to type and many new colors all of which I am sure would excite my grandmother.

When I helped her plant her bed she instructed that the seed should go in rather deep and that the soil should be well firmed. My seed catalogs advise that the nasturtium requires darkness to germinate. Whether she actually knew that I do not know but she did know that they did not germinate well if in a shallow planting. Her beds were always in full sun in light sandy soil.

I do not see the nasturtium as much as I used to. This fine old fashioned plant somehow seems to have fallen from favor. Perhaps it will be rediscovered as the plant breeders produce new varieties. Perhaps as the pendulum makes its natural swing back the Nasturtium will again claim its place.

This soft-stemmed, lush, easy to grow flower should not be overlooked or discarded. It produces a wide range of flower colors from yellow through mahogany to red. Its tender succulent leaves add a spice to your daily roughage. Whenever I see a bed or window box of nasturtiums I think, "There lives a person of character."

CHAPTER 29

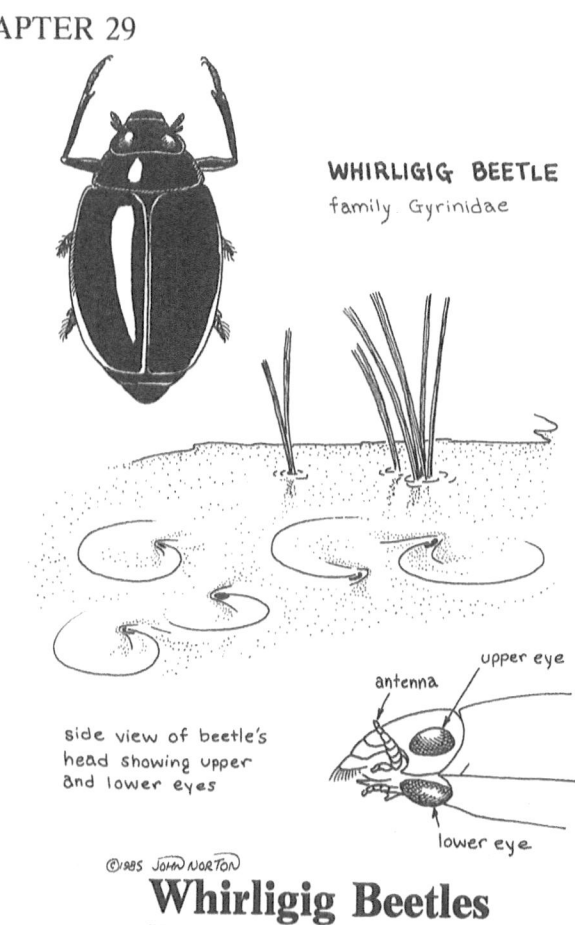

© 1985 John Norton

Whirligig Beetles
Rapid 'Swimmers'

When I was about 12 I had learned to swim sufficiently well to be allowed to go out on the Black River alone in our rowboat. This was a delicious freedom and marked the beginning of a love affair with the Black.

As the initial freedom began to be satiated, I began to notice the life that was peculiar to the river's confines. One of the earliest life forms to take my eye was the swarms of small black beetles belonging to the family *Gyrinoidea* and that they were somewhat unique in the insect world.

With a friend I spent many hours chasing these swarms of skaters. One had to row hard to catch up with a swarm which would disperse in all directions, including under the water.

Rarely did we catch a beetle and then it was difficult to keep it captured.

These little speedsters are well equipped for their niche. To begin, they are not like the water strider which skates on the surface of the water and rarely gets dunked. The whirligig beetle is partly submerged. The shiny black body has its under part under the surface. Its hind legs are broadly flattened with a dense fringe of hairs along the outer edges making them efficient paddles. The swimming movements involve a kind of feathering of the oars as they are brought forward. They are then spread out with the backward movement giving the little half-submerged boat a tremendous push resulting in astonishing speed. Their movements along the surface are a gyrating, back and forth, weaving motion. A whirligig aggregation exhibits a wide weaving pattern as it moves along with its individuals gyrating independently within the group.

The whirligig beetle is largely predacious, feeding on small animals it can capture in the water. To aid in this feeding mode it has two pairs of eyes, one for viewing above the surface of the water and the second pair for scanning the water below its surface. This glistening, black, half-inch speedboat can also fly from pond to pond as may be necessary. Thus you can find it on almost any reasonably quiet water.

There are nearly 40 beetle species that are called Whirligigs. I have no idea of what species I observed. And I guess I don't care. Tying a specific name to it is not all that important. The life cycle is typical of many insects. The female attaches her eggs to underwater bits of vegetation. The eggs hatch into tough-looking, flattened larvae which eventually leave the water and spin cocoons. After several weeks, the larval form is completely metamorphosed into the little black, oval speedsters.

One day we borrowed a fine-meshed net to capture our quarry. We were about to dip the "gigs" out of the water but they proved to be rather agile in the net, hopping out into the boat and then back into the water. Several were finally settled in a covered glass jar. After some trials we were able to feed them bits of hamburger.

I guess what I got out of this was the beginning of an appreciation for the fantastic diversity of life and the myriad adaptations that allow these forms to compete and exist. We are surrounded by incredible, miraculous bits of life which we too often take for granted.

CHAPTER 30

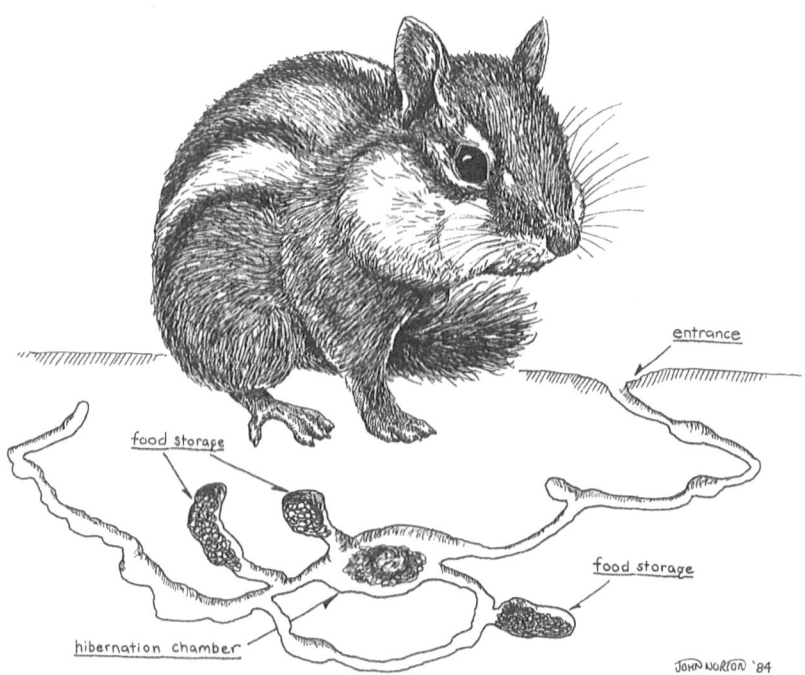

Chipmunk
Our Most Popular Rodent

Of all our resident rodents, the eastern chipmunk (*Tamis striatus*) is probably the most popular. Of our native, wild rodents it is also probably the best known. This friendly little ground squirrel can be found almost anywhere except swampy, poorly drained areas. With a little patience he easily becomes a pet and sometimes a pest.

He seems to prefer somewhat open woodlands. But if there is adequate food and shelter he will make himself at home almost anywhere as long as the drainage is adequate. His dwelling is underground. He may spend the entire winter in his subterranean apartment. This eventually gets to be quite extensive as chipmunks are always digging and improving.

Generally, very little spoil from his diggings is visible. He probably carries it away in his cheek pouches. If possible the entrance plunges straight down for a foot or so. This helps him disappear rapidly. The diggings may extend thirty feet or more. Side chambers are constructed to store food and for sleeping quarters. A fastidious animal, he constructs a special chamber for toilet use. All body wastes are deposited neatly in this special room.

A large combination bedroom-birthingroom is constructed, then lined with leaves. This may also double as a food storage room. There may be several other storage rooms. Old chipmunk burrows can get to be quite extensive and elaborate. This snug complex is home during the winter months. He sleeps a lot but does not hibernate.

In true hibernation all body processes slow down to a maintenance level. Temperature, heart rate, breathing rate all drop. The animal remains in a stupor for an extended period. This does not happen to the chipmunk. His body processes do slow down, providing a great saving in energy, but periodically he arouses himself to have a meal and then drifts back into sleep.

It is usually the male that emerges first in the spring. This greeting of the dawn of the year may occur well before the snow has vanished. However, if it has been in search of food, you may see chipmunk tracks on the snow in the dead of winter. A mild spell will often bring them above ground. By the first week in April most of the females have been bred. About a month later, blind and hairless, a half dozen or so tiny youngsters greet the world.

Mrs. *Tamis striatus* nurtures her brood alone. In six weeks or so her offspring are on their own. She may have bred again and another batch is on the way. Chipmunk food is largely vegetable matter: seeds, nuts, berries and fruits. But the occasional slug or snail, mouse, small snake or even small bird that comes its way is a welcome addition to its diet.

Late summer and early fall will find the chipmunks engaged in a frenzy of activity. They busily search every nook and cranny for seeds, nuts and the like for their winter food supply. At this time of year you are most apt to see them with cheek pouches full, scurrying into their burrows adding to the winter supplies. The volume that these cheek pouches can encompass is astounding. I once placed a large, double handful of watermelon seeds where a resident chipmunk could find them. It took just three trips to clean up the pile and store it underground.

I have many chipmunks around my home. We coexist with few problems. Occasionally they find my strawberry patch just as the berries are ripening. Then my patience wears thin. I would not begrudge them a ripe berry or two, but they seem to delight in picking half-ripened berries and arranging them neatly on the paths. Usually at this point I have to resort to trapping and releasing the miscreants "down the road a ways."

Nevertheless I value these neighbors. I enjoy watching their frolics and squabbles. They are part of the immediate food web that occupies my woods of which I am a part. They play their role, I play mine.

CHAPTER 31

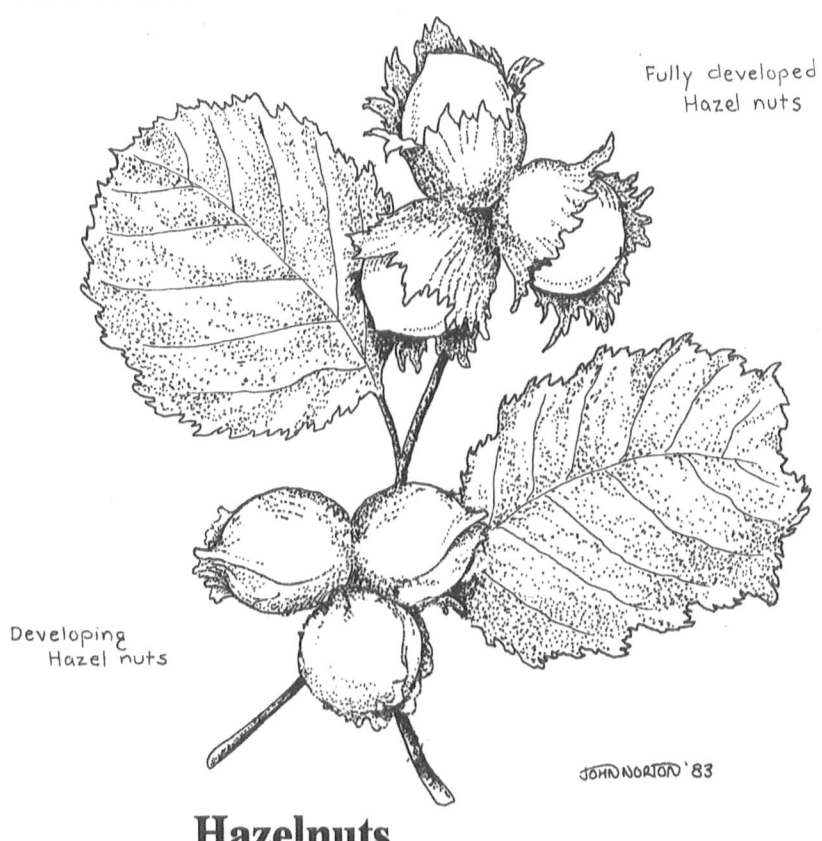

Hazelnuts
Wildlife Helps in Harvest

Years ago I received a packet of wildlife shrubs from some governmental agency. Among the several shrubs, selected for their food value to wildlife were twenty-five hazelnut, or filbert, seedlings. I carefully planted the packet envisioning that in a few years I would have some of the fruits of this planting for my own use as well as sharing with my wildlife.

My hazels thrived. Within a few yars I had a thicket of ten to twelve foot stems. These plants sucker vigorously. If conditions are favorable a single plant can eventually take over a clearing with its suckering habit. I assume that the species I have is *Corylus americana*, the American hazel, as they have survived some bitter winters that would undoubtedly have been too severe for

European varieties. The Beaked hazel, *C. Cornuta (roatrata)* is the only other American hazel native in the East. It, as the name implies, has a slender projection, or beak, on its shuck.

The American hazel produces a staminate catkin in the Fall. Catkins are drooping tassle-like spikes. In this case they produce the male sex cells necessary for fertilization. The catkins are well protected and easily survive the winter months. They are attractive to the ruffed grouse and probably some other birds. The grouse frequently come to my hazel thicket during winter's darkest weeks to feed on my catkins.

In the Spring the catkins release their pollen which is windborn to the pistillate or female flowers possibly on the same stem and reproduction is under way. I was quite anxious to gather my first crop of nuts. So the first summer after the catkins appeared I searched my thicket. I was dismayed to find that my shrubs seemed to be infected with some sort of gall.

I picked several and took them to the house to examine and see what sort of infection was afoot. I was pleasantly surprised when I cut into each gall to find a small white immature hazelnut. What I had mistaken for a gall was actually the fruit of the plant.

I did not get any nuts that year. When I judged them to be ripe they had disappeared. This happened the next year. A knowledgeable friend suggested that maybe squirrels or blue jays were harvesting them for me. I finally did get a bushel basket full which reduced to several quarts of nuts. But the problems of constantly devising new tactics to outwit my competitors has forced me to concede. My wildlife planting is now strictly for wildlife.

Actually, the nuts have now been distributed around my woods. Isolated shrubs have appeared here and there. These are frequently overlooked by my wildlife guests so that I can occasionally gather a few nuts.

In addition to squirrels and blue jays feasting on the nuts one authority states that pheasants, quail, beaver, deer and moose will add them to their diets when available. Since this wildlife planting many years ago I have found, in my wanderings, meager stands of hazelnuts here and there. But they do not seem to be common by any stretch of the imagination.

The hazelnut is a delicious nut. It is not very large, about half the size of the commercial hybrids that we purchase, but it is nevertheless a desirable fruit. It is easy to grow. It is not fussy about soil requirements. It multiplies rapidly by suckers and squirrel-planted nuts. It provides excellent food for wildlife. It is a good shrub to grow but not if you want the nuts for yourself. By carefully and continually pruning the suckers, you can persuade a single stem to become a small tree, but this requires constant vigilance. I now let my plantings grow with abandon. I now let wildlife harvest my crop with impunity. When I want hazelnuts I go to the store.

CHAPTER 32

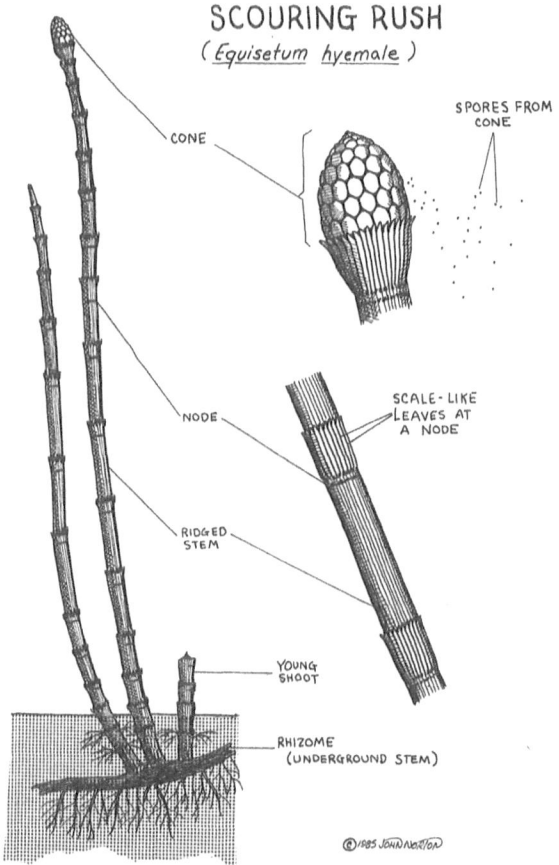

Scouring Rush
Linked to Ancient Family of Plants

From my earliest days I remember seeing on our riverbank a patch of tough, leafless plants. These plants consisted solely of dark green jointed stems that grew to about eighteen inches and were evergreen, persisting throughout the year. The hollow, jointed stems could be pulled apart in three-inch segments somewhat like the disjointing of a fly rod. The cylindrical segments were fluted and felt rough to the touch. The only leaves were a small fringe at each node. Apparently, the food making process, photosynthesis, was concentrated in the stems.

This unusual plant, the scouring rush (*Equisetum hiemale*), is one of about twenty-five species, the only remnants of an ancient plant group. During the Paleozoic era, 180-500 million years ago, this family grew in gigantic forests covering the land surface on the earth. It is the remains of these primitive plants that constitute the bulk of the world's coal deposits.

It was a few years later that I became acquainted with the name, scouring rush. A friend told me that with a wad of scouring rush, some wood ashes and a measure of elbow grease, one could clean the worst frying pan. I tried the technique on subsequent scouting trips and found it effective, especially when the measure of elbow grease used was large.

From the top of some of the stems grows a cone-like structure which produces spores from May through September. This primitive reproductive mode is indicative of the ancient nature of the plant. The scouring rush may be found throughout Canada and the United States. It seems to tolerate a wide variety of soils but prefers sandy soils. It prefers a neutral soil. If the soil is sweet or sour the polishing grass will not do well. It may be found in dry as well as moist areas. Under optimum conditions it may reach three feet in height.

Silica is the major ingredient in most sand. The scouring action of the scouring rush comes from the silica that is in the stalk skin. Thus a tough abrasive is embedded in the stem. At one time this form of fine sandpaper was used by woodworkers. The name shave grass probably reflects this use.

Many years ago I was showing a music teacher a patch of scouring rush. He examined one of the stem sections and with surprise informed me that these cylinders, when dried, were used to fashion the reeds used with oboes, bassoons and other reed instruments. "You could make a lot of money selling these," he said. Reflecting on the limited number of oboe players and bassoonists, I decided that I would seek my fortune elsewhere.

The plant world contains plants that range through all degrees of complexity. Somewhere near the bottom of the complexity scale is the scouring rush. Complexity and sophistication are not necessary for success. Though it retains the simplicity of its ancestors, *Equisetum hiemale* has persisted through millions of years. In the biological world this is evidence of success. I wonder, is there not a lesson for us, mankind, in this?

CHAPTER 33

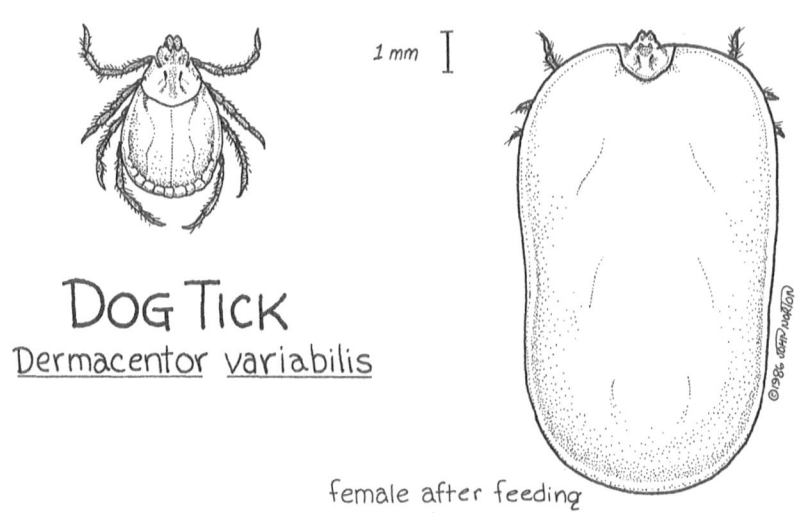

DOG TICK
Dermacentor variabilis

female after feeding

Ticks
Unwelcome Guests

I was enjoying the company of a nice little dog. It was a hot day in August. My canine friend was playful and so was I. I became aware that sometimes as I scratched his ears and neck he seemed to wince as if in pain. So I took a good look. Just ahead of his collar was a large blue-black lump nearly the size of a small walnut. It seemed to be attached by a narrow isthmus. When I touched it my companion pulled away.

I had discovered a tick. It was so distended with blood that it appeared to have no body features other than its nut-like shape. A gentle tug made my friend whimper. The tick was attached by its jaws buried in my little comrade's skin. Pulling it off might leave behind the head with the imbedded jaws and result in an infection. A swab of alcohol did not seem to be persuasive enough. A drop of turpentine did the trick. The tick backed off and dropped into the palm of my hand. It was egg-shaped, easily three-quarters of an inch long and nearly as wide.

The life cycle of this animal is such to make its survival seem impossible. But nature makes provision for her children and the tick is no exception. The tick life cycle goes through four stages. First the egg, one of several thousand that the female has deposited on the ground, hatches into a larva. The first thing this form must do is catch a meal. Sensitive and attracted to light, the tiny four-legged larva crawls to the tip of nearby grass or other vegetation. Hanging from the tallest point it can find, it waits for a passing animal.

As an animal approaches, the tick larva begins wildly to wave its front pair of legs. Some species appear to be able to detect the presence of a host at some distance. At the slightest touch of the prospective host the tick lets go its perch and burrows down through the hair to the skin for the first of the three meals it will have during its lifetime.

After a few days, engorged with blood, it drops to the ground. It now avoids light and hides while it digests its meal and begins to change into a third stage, the eight-legged nymph. This may be in several weeks or, if winter approaches, the following spring.

Ravenous, it repeats the previous performance and finds another host. Again it dines. Again it drops back to the ground. Again it changes form, this time into an adult. And once again it must find a meal, the third and last. Once fed, the female searches the body of her host for a mate. With mating completed she drops to the ground to lay enormous numbers of eggs and the cycle starts anew. The cycle may take two or more years and the adult can live up to three years. In the laboratory, ticks have been kept alive for five years. It would seem that this complicated life cycle would work against the tick's survival. But patience and the ability to exist for long periods without food insure that the species will be perpetuated.

Just about every living thing has its parasite. The human creature is no exception. We are subject to many parasites which range from the microscopic to the highly visible. About this time of year the tick seems to come into prominence. Mammals are the most likely hosts. However, there are tick species that prefer birds and some species that use cold blooded animals. Ticks transmit to humans several rather serious diseases. After an afternoon in the field with your dog, you should carefully examine the dog and yourself to insure that you aren't in the bed and breakfast business for a transient tick.

CHAPTER 34

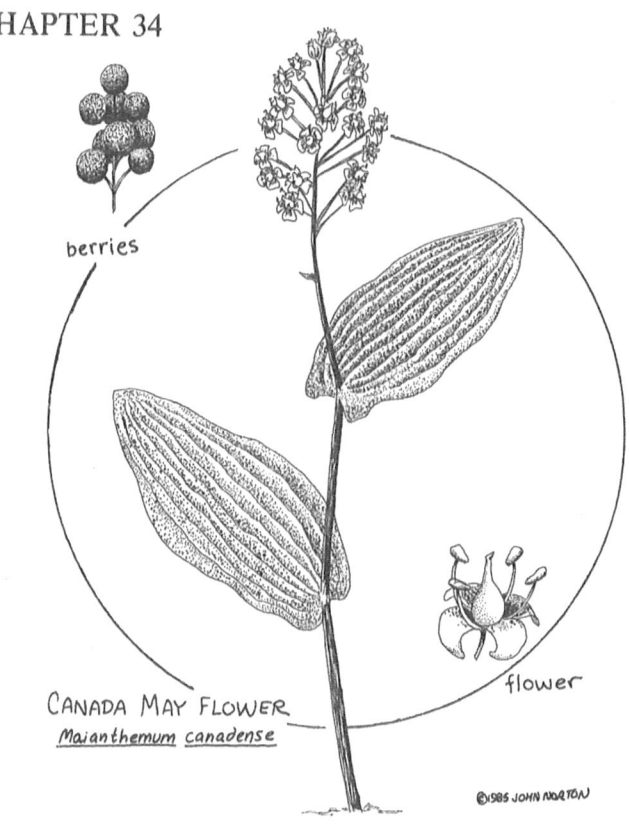

Mayflower
A Tiny Gem

In late April or early May large patches of my woods begin to show a faint blush of green. The normally brown pine duff slowly shows a green wash that intensifies each day.

As the end of May approaches these patches become a thick mat of small, low, green plants. In June the green is diluted with hundreds of delicate white flowers. Each blossom gives off a delicate perfume. So faint is this scent that I can't detect it from a single bloom. But when walking downwind of a large patch, this delightful perfume is quite evident.

These large patches of this delicate flower contain hundreds, perhaps thousands, of the Canada Mayflower or Wild Lily-of-the-Valley (*Maianthemum canadense*). The Canada Mayflower is widely distributed in North America from Labrador to British

Columbia south to Tennessee and into the mountains of Georgia. It is a low growing flower perhaps three to six inches in height.

The leaves are interesting in that they are stalkless. The base is indented so that from a distance the stem appears to be growing right through the leaf. The young plant will probably have only one leaf. The mature plant may have three leaves. It belongs to the lily family, the members of which display their flower parts in numbers of three or six.

Here again the Wild Lily-of-the-Valley displays an interesting variation in that its flower plan is based on four. Its blossom has four stamens, four sepals and four petals. Actually, what goes for a blossom is an aggregation of flowers along the stalk, each flower having its own tiny separate stalk. This design is called a raceme.

This delicate, diminutive piece of creation is very fragile. One has to walk through a bed only two or three times to find that the beginnings of a path have been formed. I carefully keep to the established paths and cringe when my dog races through the velvet green carpet.

In my early days, to be beautiful a flower had to be large. Beautiful was big. Tulips, sunflowers, trilliums fitted the definition. I rarely noticed the smaller flowers although my mother continually called my attention to the various bits of elegance we came across in our wanderings. Somewhere along the line I acquired small traces of maturity. My maturity has never been steady or extensive. It has always come to me in small bits and has never kept up with my chronological development.

Nevertheless, I began to see that beauty was all around me, that it was packaged in many different sizes, that its form was myriad. The Canada Mayflower is a perfect example of Lilliputian elegance.

Some years the green carpets persist all through the summer months. Most of the time beginning in July the leaves begin to turn brown and soon the entire patch fades into the duff except for many tiny red fruits that adorn the blossom stalk. Initially this berry is grey gradually turning into a bright red. Each of these berries contains one or two seeds.

Our world contains many things of beauty. The mighty mountain is offset by the tiny hummingbird. The majestic waterfall is balanced by the diminutive Canada mayflower. Most of the things of beauty are small. Perhaps if I live long enough I may be able to truly appreciate these countless tiny gems.

CHAPTER 35

Song Sparrow
Song a Rhapsody

The song sparrow, in its several geographical variations, is one of the most widely known and recognized of the many sparrows. It goes by many names. The esteem in which it is held is indicated by two of these names, silver tongue and everybody's darling. It is one of my favorite sparrows because of its beautiful singing.

When silver tongue sings he does it with all his being. He mounts his singing post, throws his head back, angles his bill to the sky and pours out his magic. It is magic to me at least. The worst possible day in the world can be tempered by everybody's darling. When I hear his song things are bound to take a turn for the better.

The sexes in this six and a half inch bird are identical in appearance. The back is a chestnut brown streaked with black. The underparts are white with black streaks. The blotches on the highly streaked breast converge to form a dark spot similar to the tree sparrow. This is probably the most distinguishing characteristic, streaked breast with a dark spot. A slightly forked tail is also useful in identification.

These songsters appear in March to begin their singing. Once silver tongue has staked out a territory the singing becomes profuse. He establishes several singing perches and moves from one to another announcing to all the world that he is ready for business.

As soon as a suitable mate appears and the pairing has been established the nest building commences. Most of the time the nest is located on the ground under a tuft of grass. Ground nesters are subject to considerable predation. The year or two that we had cats we had no song sparrows. It was only after the cats left that everybody's darling returned to favor me with his music.

In the nest, constructed of fine grasses, weed stems and leaves, are deposited four or five eggs. These pale green, dark-splotched eggs are incubated by the female for 10 to 14 days. Both parents participate in feeding the brood. By fall the young have developed so that they are practically indistinguishable from their parents.

Since silver tongue prefers open areas I do not have much suitable habitat for him nearby. Usually I feel fortunate if a pair chooses to nest in my clearing. There are areas that I no longer mow in hopes of enticing him into residency.

The bulk of his food is weed seeds. A substantial portion, probably a third, is insects. So he is a useful bird. But it is his music that endears him to everybody. He has many variations, but it is the ebullient, bubbling, torrent that fills the air which identifies him.

One spring, years ago, a songster perched each morning in a tree by my bedroom window. For five to ten minutes he filled the air with delightful variations proclaiming that the rebirth of the year was imminent. It was a tonic that started me on each day's duties. Now, sometimes when I hear silver tongue I am transported back to those days when youth was supreme.

So, the song sparrow, *Melospiza melodia*, ranks high in my book. He does not have much in the way of colorful plumage but he is way ahead in song.

CHAPTER 36

Eastern Worm Snake
Carpophis amoenus

Eastern Worm Snake
Gentle, Harmless

One fall after a severe frost I was spading a portion of my garden. I turned over a shovel of soil to unearth a tiny, tight, coral coil. The color was beautiful, a delicate pastel, pink-coral. At first I thought it was an earring that one of my offspring had lost. I picked it up to discover that I had been looking at the belly surface of a dainty little snake, which probably was curled as a result of the cold.

The back or dorsal surface of this delicate little animal was a dark brown. The pink from the bottom, the ventral surface, continued up its side one or two rows of scales. Its head was more pointed than most snakes. I took my find into the house and went for the snake book. I finally decided that I had found an Eastern worm snake (*Carphophis amoenus amoenus*). One source shows the range of these reptiles as barely touching New York along the southern Hudson valley. Another source states they are found north to southern New England.

The name worm snake comes from the fact that it does resemble the common earthworm in looks, and more so in habit, as it burrows into soft earth. It spends much of its time underground and in times of drought will penetrate deeply into the earth to avoid dehydration. Its food consists mainly of earthworms and insects.

As the warmth of my hand penetrated the little body it began to move and suddenly was very active. It squirmed around my fingers until it became difficult to hold it without injuring it. So I put it in a glass jar and took it outside. The sun was now high and the day warm. I put the little jewel near a wood pile and hoped that it would make it through the winter.

In the years since I first became acquainted with this beautiful little animal I have found him many times. He is a gentle, harmless creature. During the times I have handled him he has never shown me any agressive behavior. Should you come across him admire him but do him no harm. Let him go about the business of living unmolested. Surely you can't begrudge him his place in life's scheme. If the term snake bothers you, think worm.

CHAPTER 37

Red-Tailed Hawk
Gets Bad Press

Years ago when every farm had its flock of chickens, as did many townspeople, the sight of the graceful soaring of the red-tailed hawk would bring cries of "chicken hawk" or "hen hawk." Shotguns would come out. The air would be filled with holes and resound with the sounds of gunshots. As with many of nature's phenomena, man got off on the wrong foot. In the mistaken belief that hawks lived on chickens, any and all of the raptors, the birds of prey, were indiscriminately slaughtered. As a result, in my early days, hawks were not very common.

But there has been a change. We have become more enlightened, as surely we must if we are to survive. More and more we have begun to see the place that the raptors have in the scheme of things. These magnificent birds play a key role. Nature's act is one of balance, and the red-tailed hawk occupies an important place on one side of the scale.

Now I often see the red-tailed hawk, as well as other hawks. I now hear his shrill kree-ee-ee and watch his aerial maneuverings frequently. As the name implies this hawk has a red tail. But the tail is red on the upper side only. Since we are most apt to see him soaring overhead this red is often difficult to detect.

However, if you watch his twistings and turnings carefully you will eventually catch a glimpse of the rufous-red tail feathers. Sometimes, if the light above is strong, a reddish glint will show through to the observer below.

The red-tailed hawk belongs to a group of raptors called Buteos. These are large birds. When viewed from below they show large rounded wings and large rounded tails. They soar high in the sky in lazy circles which probably earned them the name Buzzard hawks.

Red does a lot of perching. You may frequently find him perched on a tall tree in forested areas with open patches in view. The major portion of his diet consists of rodents, chipmunks, mice, squirrels and rats. He also takes a few small birds, snakes, woodchucks, muskrats and rabbits. So he rests where he can scan for food.

The nest is also located in forested areas. The kind of tree does not seem to be as important as is the height. One of the higher trees in a tract will be selected as the nest tree. Sometimes the pair will use the same nest for several years. Sometimes a new site will be selected each year in the same area. If the same nest is used its size increases each year.

These nests of sticks can get to be several feet in diameter. The platform is constructed of rather large sticks. Once the base is finished the central depression is lined with smaller sticks and twigs. The nest will be decorated with bits of pine or hemlock or other greenery. Sometimes you can tell if a nest is occupied by these green decorations. Mrs. Red will deposit two to four eggs in this abode. They will vary greatly in shape and decoration.

Late one June afternoon I was seated at the upper edge of a sloping meadow. The several acres of tall grasses were surrounded on three sides with thick forest growth. Somewhere behind me was a grove of large white pines. In the distance the Black River made a silver ribbon as it wound down the valley. Suddenly out of nowhere a hawk dropped into the waving grass. Just as quickly it was up and out with a meadow mouse in its talons. Almost as quickly another hawk performed the same act a few yards away.

During the next hour or so the pair made a half dozen raids into the tall grass. I was well enough concealed so that to their keen eyes I represented no threat. One foray resulted in considerable thrashing in the grass. The hawk finally arose without its prey. I assumed that it had unsuccessfully tried to take a woodchuck. Not wishing to put an end to the drama, I did not dare rise from my concealment but later as I walked through the tall grass I did find a large woodchuck mound.

The red-tailed hawk (*Buteo jamaicensis*) has a number of variant races throughout the continent concentrated largely in Eastern North America. It is probably the hawk that most of us see. Certainly it is becoming more common.

More and more we are able to thrill to the soaring of this magnificent bird that has returned from the ravages of the shotgun and DDT. There is hope. Our blindness to nature's ways is being relieved. Slowly our sight is being restored. Perhaps someday coexistence rather than conquer will be the watchword.

CHAPTER 38

Take a Lesson From Red Hen

The first story I ever read completely by myself was *The Little Red Hen*. It was probably during the first grade. My mother had begun to teach me to read before I went to school so I was ready and anxious. The idea of reading a story, then a book, and ultimately a newspaper, loomed high in my desires. I clearly recall envying adults who could sit down for interminable lengths of time with nothing else but a book or newspaper.

In all probability rote memory played an important part in this first reading success. The story had been read to me many times. We had a copy of The Primer in The Winston Readers series. My mother went over the words with me again and again. I probably could have recited the entire story had such a performance been necessary. "Not I," said the cat. "Not I," said the goose. "Not I," said the pig." I remember these sentences rolling out with delicious abandon. I can recall the total satisfaction as I turned the pages and read the story the first time.

My offspring are familiar with the story, although they have never seen the book, as I have talked about it many times. I suspect very few individuals under fifty know much about this marvelous hen. Perhaps they "teethed" on something else that is just as precious.

The story is simple as are all good stories. The little red hen acquired some wheat which she wished to plant. She asked some of the farmyard animals for help but was rebuffed. The story read, "'Then I will plant the wheat,' said the Little Red Hen. And she did." Requests for help at harvest time were similarly without results. The grinding of the wheat into flour was accomplished alone as was the ultimate bread baking. Each episode ended with the hen saying that she would do the job herself. "And she did."

Consuming the final product, the golden loaves of bread, was a different story. All the animals volunteered to help. But since they had not helped, the little red hen shared the bread only with her chicks.

The moral of the story takes a number of forms. "There is no free lunch." "You don't get something for nothing." "You only get what you pay for." Even "Help thy neighbor," applies. The moral was not lost on me. We even enlarged it to include helping someone without thought of reward. My mother stressed the satisfaction of just helping someone.

The story can easily be rewritten with endless substitutions making it most applicable in today's world. Substitute for the gentle hen; the volunteer fire department, the United Fund, the Heart Association, Save the Whales, your local historical society and hundreds of other worthwhile endeavors. The recalcitrant farm animals are those of us who contribute nothing, or who belong but do nothing but criticize, or who do not even lend our names but who practice the privilege of criticism along with doing nothing.

Fortunately there are in our society substantial numbers of red hens. Unfortunately, as in the story, there are even greater numbers of "farm animals," dogs, cats and geese, whose motto is "Not I." Too many of us are content to sit back and "let George do it." My plea is that more of us make the effort to become red hens. "And she did."

CHAPTER 39

Heron
Our Stately Bird

During my high school days I spent many hours on the Black River. I fished a lot but frequently would just allow the boat to drift watching the shoreline and the abundant life that existed there. One day while with a companion we were alerted by a commotion at the water's edge on the opposite shore. Upon investigation it proved to be a Great Blue Heron. As we approached, it floundered in the water and we could see that it had something in its bill.

Closer examination showed that it had speared a bullhead which remained stuck on its bill. The bill had pierced the thick skull of the bullhead trapping the bird. We decided we would free the bird from its trap, but as we approached we had second thoughts. Even in its weakened condition the powerful wings seemed formidable. Even with the bullhead attached to its rapier bill it seemed prudent to stand our distance. We had an old blanket folded on a seat in the boat which we spread and threw over the bird. With the bird thus hampered we were able to wrap the blanket around the wings and gain access to the head.

The bullhead was solidly wedged on to the bill. It required some force to relieve the bird. Once freed we were faced with the problem of how to let the bird go. I was not anxious to place myself within thrusting range of the sharp bill or the pounding radius of the thumping large wings. We finally wrapped the bird, head and all, in the blanket and laid it on the shore. With a length of rope tied to a corner of the blanket we gently pulled the blanket free. Our bird slowly got on its feet and moved into the cattails. We hoped it would soon find a frog or fish as it was obvious it had not eaten in some time.

Largest Heron

This stately bird is the largest of our herons. Its length can go over four feet, the legs easily three feet or better and the wingspread tops six feet. It is extremely wary and to observe it closely requires considerable stalking skill. But your patience will be well rewarded.

Standing absolutely motionless with its long neck retracted in an "S" curve it patiently waits for its prey to come within range. It knows the arc within which it can successfully capture the unwary frog or minnow. As soon as the quarry is within range the neck straightens, the bill snaps and the meal is on its way down the long gullet. It is not generally known that the Great Blue Heron also feasts on field mice providing a considerable measure of rodent control in some areas.

This regal, silent, stalker moves with a deliberate slow-motion precision that is beautiful to watch. Slowly it lifts an incredibly long leg. If the water is shallow the foot is held momentarily with a toe still beneath the surface so that the water will not drip giving the position away. With the water drained off, the foot is slowly lifted, moved forward and gently reinserted into the water. Not a ripple disturbs the surface to alert the cautious frog. Not a sound ensues to warn the careless sunfish.

No mud swirls around its feet to caution the dozing tadpole. If the water is deep the foot is carefully eased forward beneath the surface with incredible finesse keeping the calm of the pool intact.

The Great Blues are gregarious only during the nesting season. When proper conditions exist they gather together in rookeries. There may be over a hundred nests in one of these heronries with sometimes several nests in a single tree. However, many birds nest in isolation with a single nest far away from other nesting pairs. The nests are large bulky affairs made of sticks and twigs. Three to six blue-green eggs comprise the clutch. The adults are good parents feeding the fledglings regurgitated delicacies. The parents take turns incubating the eggs with the free bird feeding the incubating partner choice regurgitations. Widely distributed, it breeds over most of the United States and Canada, wintering in the middle states south through Central America.

The flight of the Great Blue is a dignified, stately, measured movement through the air. The long neck is curved back producing a great downward keel-like bend with the head pulled back. Once in flight its long legs angle straight toward the rear. Because of its size its speed is deceptive. It does not seem to move very fast. But its steady rowing will soon put it out of your sight.

Great it is but blue it is not. At least not blue in the sense of a bluebird or a blue jay. Slatey blue or battleship grey is perhaps more apt, with considerable white and plain grey. But whatever the color this majestic bird deserves as much attention as does the cardinal or the tanager.

Appearing initially to be gaunt and awkward the Great Blue is in every sense a stately, dignified and graceful bird. He is relatively common if you only look. You may not have a marsh nearby to tempt him. But if you scan the skies you will frequently see him as he moves with flowing precision toward the horizon.

CHAPTER 40

Balsam
Smells Woodsy

Nature is full of delightful (and not so delightful) scents. From the very first we are exposed to a myriad of smells, most of which escape us. Some, however, perhaps because of their extreme delightfulness or perhaps through repetition, repeated exposure, remain fixed in our odor memory.

A whiff of some certain aroma can release the flood of nostalgia. Sometimes we can identify the scent and the incident. Sometimes the incident flashes to mind but the scent's identity remains hidden. But it can be powerful.

One such scent, for me, is the clean smell of balsam. It goes way back with me. Our early Christmas trees were balsams. At that time the pines were not in fashion. Spruce or balsam graced our living room. Spruce quickly lost its needles. Balsam held its needles for weeks if needed. So for that reason balsam was favored. But the house filled with balsam scent was what sold most people on this graceful evergreen. All I need is a whiff of balsam and I can go way back.

But the scent of balsam was not confined to the holiday season. Our home had, as did many homes at that time, a balsam pillow. About 8 by 10 by 5 or 6 inches, this bag of scent poured forth its delight day and night, year after year.

Some dedicated soul stripped the needles off armfuls of balsam branches to the tune of about two quarts. These were stuffed into the bag and the opening sewed shut. No great technology was involved here. No great scientific principle was discovered and put to use. It was only a simple (granted tedious) harvesting and stuffing operation. But the result, a lasting treasure of woodsy aroma. Something that gave for years.

We still have the pillow. The balsam needles are bone dry and mostly reduced to a powder. But they still produce their magic. I bury my nose and inhale. There is still the faint scent of those conifer leaves picked so long ago. I inhale again and am transported back to a summer evening on our front porch. Nestled on a cot with the balsam pillow I ride out a mighty thunder storm. I do not know when my parents acquired the pillow but it must have been 60 to 70 years ago.

Some years ago I thought to replace the old needles with a fresh harvest. I envisioned deep draughts of fresh, strong balsam scent. I gathered several large armloads of balsam branches and proceeded to strip the needles. Stripping against the grain with my fingers was only partially successful. A small pen knife was more efficient. A pair of wire stripping pliers was a disappointment.

After considerable time I was surrounded with piles of stripped branches but the result was only two or three cupfuls of the small aromatic needles. It was quite apparent that I needed many, many more armfuls of branches and several days of stripping to harvest enough needles for the pillow I had in mind. Other events intruded. The project was laid aside. Several years have passed. I do not yet have my new pillow but I do have an increased appreciation for the work that went into our old balsam pillow.

CHAPTER 41

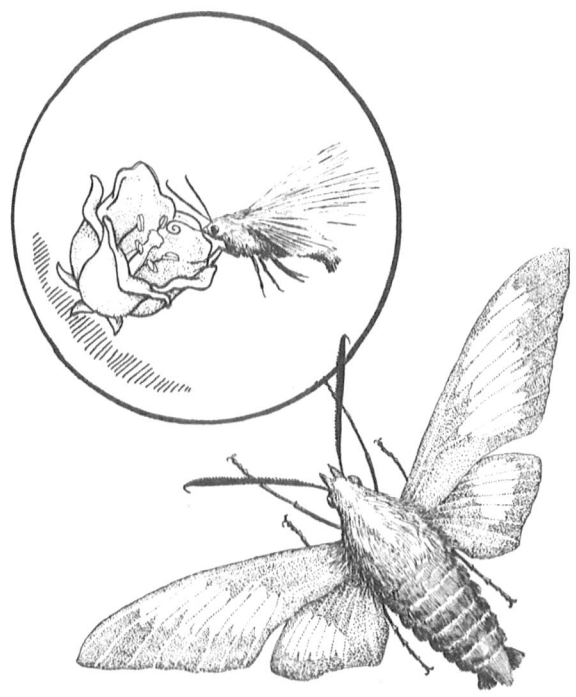

HUMMINGBIRD MOTH
Hemaris thysbe

©1984 JOHN MORTON

Hummingbird Moth
Fascinating Flyer

When I was young, a portion of my mother's garden contained a bed of a perennial she called rocket. These white through pink to purple flowers bloomed in profusion, produced a delicate perfume and were very attractive to many insects.

One of the very first jobs I can remember was that of cutting the heads of these plants as the blooms faded. This would induce a second crop of blossoms. Armed with a pair of blunt-nosed scissors I would go each day and cut off those stalks that I considered past their bloom. One time late in the day I became aware of a soft humming sound in the nearby flowers. I was hearing the soft murmur of the hummingbird moth.

The hummingbird moth, *Hermaris thysbe*, is active during daylight hours wherever there is an abundance of nectar. It is sometimes called the clear-winged moth because of large areas on its wings that are devoid of scales and thus transparent. While these interesting little moths belong to the same family as the sphinx or tomato or hornworm moth they are not a garden pest.

Most abundant in June and July, they mate and produce a light green larval form that eventually pupates and spends the winter on the ground in a cocoon. As the name implies, this insect hovers and maneuvers like the hummingbird. It is not as wary as the hummingbird and is relatively easy to watch.

The hind wings are very much smaller than the forewings. The relatively large body is covered with hairy scales and has a conspicuous tuft of hairs at the posterior end of the abdomen.

At first I was wary of this little hummer. I thought that the humming sound might be the warning of a stinging insect. After I was assured that it was harmless I began to watch it closely and eventually caught a specimen. Placed under a large glass jar it had sufficient room to fly. Ensconced on the kitchen table it buzzed and hummed allowing my mother and I to watch its aerial stunts. After a while she would suggest that it probably needed feeding and should be released. So back to the garden it would go. As I recall I repeated this sequence several times.

I spent many happy hours watching these fascinating little flyers. In recent years I have not seen them with any frequency. Perhaps it is because I do not have the flowers that they frequent. Or perhaps it is because my garden is isolated and they have not found me. I hope it is not that they are scarce because of environmental stress.

CHAPTER 42

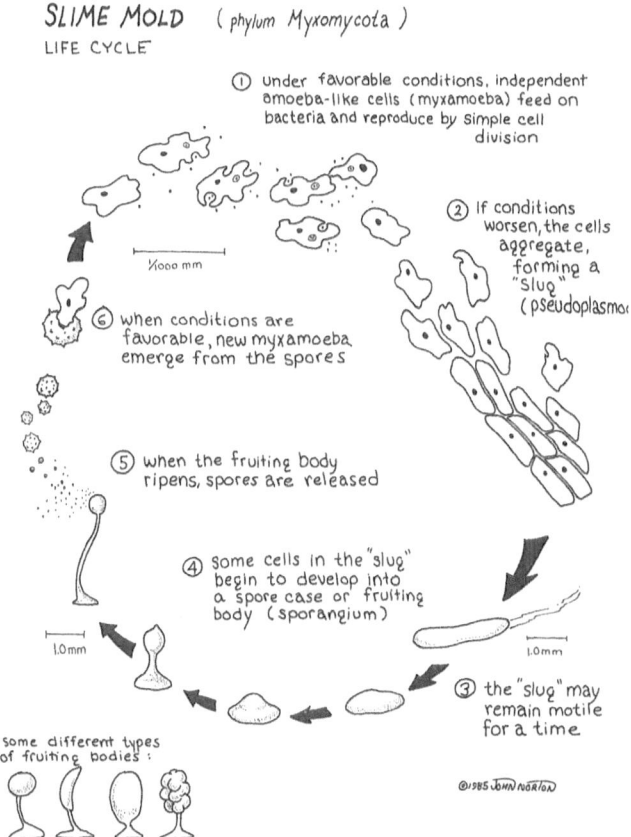

Slime Mold
Backyard Drama

"Blauugh," you say with your tongue sticking out, mustering all the disgust at your command, when I show you a glistening, white, slippery, gelatinous mass on the underside of a board in your yard. Well, I'm not asking you to eat it. I just want you to look at it carefully. We turn over a layer of old dead leaves to find a delicate orange blob. Looking at it carefully we see that it appears to have a network of veins. Looking at our discoveries some time later we find that they have moved.

These strange blobs are among the most fascinating organisms you are apt to encounter in your yard or nearby fields. During a very humid summer these slime molds, for that is what they are called, are found almost everywhere there is decaying vegetation. The slime mold stage that we see comes in many colors; red, orange, yellow, brown, gray and white. This stage is the end, or perhaps the beginning, of a fascinating cycle most of which is not visible to the naked eye.

If your eyes had the magnification of a microscope and you could look at a moist patch of decaying leaves you might see a large number of rather widely separated grazing organisms. These almost colorless bodies are single cells that handily take care of all their needs with a quiet efficiency. Each of these single cells moves along amoeba-like ingesting bacteria that it finds on the decaying materials that cover the ground.

This quiet feasting will continue until suddenly a signal is received. Each cell now seems to have been imbued with a purpose. A migration begins. The scattering of millions and millions of separate cells, if enlarged to human size, would have individuals perhaps miles from each other. Somehow, a message is sent and received and the scattering begins to converge on a rendezvous.

As the grazing herd turns, it continues to feed on bacteria that chance its path. Individuals begin to come together. They join and merge. Streaming paths converge and consolidate. An organization takes place. Different cells take on specialized duties. Ingested food is now carried along special pathways much the way digested food is distributed in our bodies. The conglomeration of single cells had become an entity in itself. It is a multicellular organism.

It now has the shape of a vast sheet. The sheet is organized. It is coordinated, its individual cells obeying some central command. As the sheet flows over the terrain something guides and directs it. As it moves it engulfs nutritional materials which flow toward a centralized point through vein-like tubes. At some point this glistening, slightly undulating sheet, which now may be six inches across, slows its relentless travel.

Again a major signal is given and received. A bump appears at the conjunction of the highway-like veins. The bump swells and begins to elongate vertically. A stalk grows until it projects well above the seething mass below. Trying to translate this again into human terms would put this tower up many stories in the air.

Something comparable to the Empire State building is being constructed.

The top of the tower begins to form a ball-like structure. It changes color and darkens. Individual cell-like forms become apparent. In the meantime the edges of the once vigorous sheet below begin to shrivel. Activity slows. The stalk begins to wither as from its rounded top a storm of dark spores is shed. The organism is dying. At the same time it is being reborn. Air currents distribute this discharge far and wide. The dormant spores eventually fall to earth to wait quietly for favorable conditions that will include activation. And the cycle begins again.

Science fiction? No, this is real. And the drama occurs whenever conditions of warmth, moisture and food supplies are available. Your backyard probably has its supply of slime molds. Almost any woodland area, roadside ditch or weedpatch will feature this incredible performance. All you have to do is look for it.

CHAPTER 43

NORTHERN WHITE CEDAR
Thuja occidentalis

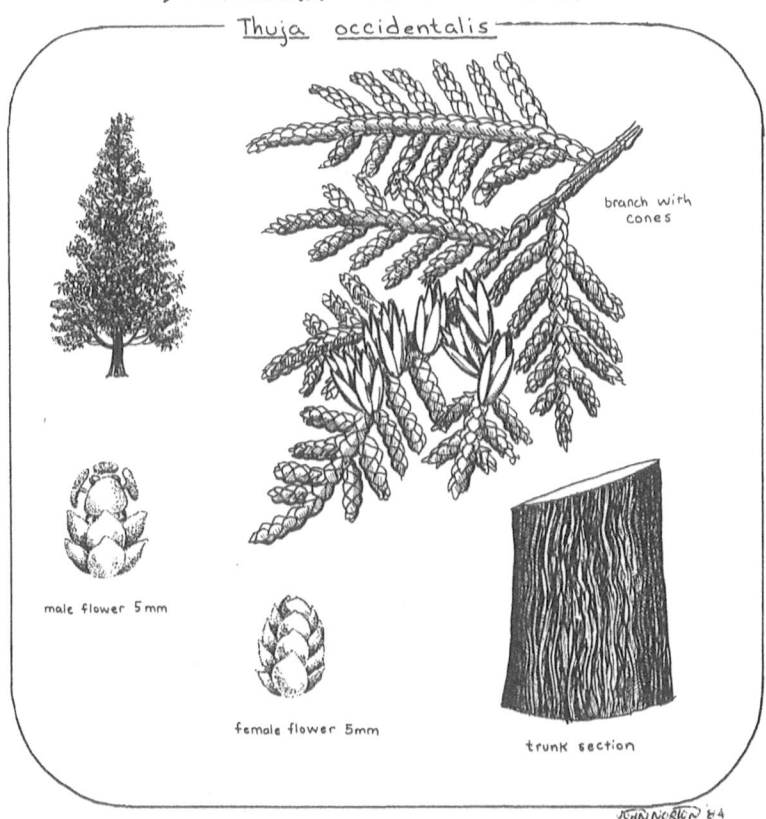

Northern White Cedar
Arborvitae

One of my favorite trees is the Northern White Cedar (*Thuja occidentalis*). Known to most as just cedar it also goes by the name of arborvitae. This evergreen is limited to the Northern Lake States, New England and Canada, with a slender band flourishing down along the central Appalachians. It likes the cold. It grows in poorly drained soils. Who hasn't heard of a cedar swamp? But is also does well on well-drained soils, especially limestone areas, as long as plenty of water is available to the root system.

Its twigs and branchlets are unique in that they are covered by overlapping pairs of tightly fitting green scales. These pairs fit at right angles to each other along the stem producing a beautiful woven effect. The twigs branch out in a single plane somewhat parallel to the ground. This produces an attractive fern-like frond. The cones, for it is a conifer, appear on the twigs in an upright position. Arborvitae is monoecious. That is, each plant bears imperfect male and female blossoms.

In addition to its yearlong, attractive greenery it features a delightful scent. This is not to be confused with the pleasing odor of the cedar chest, which comes from the red cedars. The aroma of the northern white cedar is "cedarish." It suggests cedar but is different, somewhat more delicate. Crush some cedar twigs in your hand and hold them up to your nose. You will savor an olfactory representation of the whole outdoors.

If growing in the open it can produce an impressive conical, compact stem of up to fifty or sixty feet with a diameter of two to three feet. Arborvitae is the substance of most hedges in the north country. It shears well and quickly forms a dense compact barrier. It is easily propagated from cuttings and because of its compact root system transplants well.

White cedar is a light wood both in color and density. It resists decay and consequently is widely used for fence posts, shingles and the like. Years ago we made some duck decoys out of white cedar. The wood was soft and easily worked. They turned out reasonably well. But we liked them especially as they were easy to carry. A packbasket full of decoys was easily transported back and forth to some secret Adirondack Pond. This was greatly appreciated at the end of the day when everything had increased its weight by several hundred percent.

Cedar makes a fine winter browse for deer. When winter snows are deep the deer retreat to cedar yards. Two or three pounds of cedar browse each day will carry a deer through the most difficult of winters. If more is available and easily obtained they might even gain weight.

Thus, this rather common tree, familiar to many, yet really well-known by few, merits your attention. The next time you have the opportunity, examine an arborvitae twig. Look at the exquisite design which has been described as "one of the most artistic designs discovered on the twigs of any tree in the world." Savor the scent of the freshly crushed twig. Admire the dense, compact shape and the yearlong yellow-green of its finery. The sum of these will convince you that this is an outstanding tree.

CHAPTER 44

PARASOL MUSHROOM
Macrolepiota procera

Parasol Mushroom
Can Be a Real Treat

Every day you see thousands and thousands of species of fungi. These are but a miniscule fraction of the total number of these organisms that are in existence. Fungi range in size from the tiny, microscopic yeasts to the giant puffball that may weigh 100 pounds or more.

Unlike green plants, and like animals, fungi cannot synthesize their own food requirements. Since, unlike animals, they are immobile, they must be closely associated with their food supply. A majority of fungi species are saprophytes in that they live off dead organisms. Some are parasitic in that they get their nourishment from living organisms.

Probably the best known fungi are mushrooms. What we see and call the mushroom is actually the fruiting body of the organism that is appearing after perhaps several years of undetected growth. This fruiting body releases billions of spores. Launched into the air currents, these tiny spores sometimes drift incredible distances. Very few spores find circumstances favorable for germination.

As a youngster barely able to carry the mushroom basket I was introduced to mushrooms. Both my father and mother picked the little tan fairy ring from our lawn. After several years of apprenticeship I was allowed to help with the harvest.

Over the years I have become comfortable with a dozen or so varieties, familiar with several times that many, and learned to shun all the rest. One of the species I use when it is available is the parasol mushroom, *Leucoagaricus procerus*. This aptly named mushroom is quite large. I have harvested some that were nearly a foot in diameter, from a stalk over a foot tall, and unquestionably looking very much like a parasol.

The parasol button appears from a swollen bulb-like base. Initially the button and its stalk are covered by brownish spots. As the button expands into the cap, expansion breaks the brown into wood-colored, shaggy scales. As the cap breaks away from the stalk a ring remains that is movable up and down, like a bracelet. The gills under the cap area are white with occasionally a faint pink wash. They do not touch the stem and produce a white spore.

I do not find this delectable fruit in profusion. It comes up in my lawn and in some open areas in my woods. If I harvest a half dozen at a time I am doing well. Sometimes there are not enough for a meal. This is no problem as the parasol mushroom dries easily and can be stored until enough are harvested for a feast. Also this fine mushroom is not as readily susceptible to worm invasions as are other mushrooms.

If I do not have enough I string them on a thread from the ceiling until I am ready to use them. A brief soaking in water reconstitutes these delicacies. They are cooked as you would any mushroom. Mushroom fanciers rate the parasol as one of the best.

I recall one memorable evening when I toasted several parasols by a campfire to complete a fantastic day.

I usually find the parasol after a good rain in late summer and fall. Usually it grows singly; only rarely do I find clumps. When I find the first one I make the rounds to spots where I found them previously. If you like mushrooms, you will certainly go for the parasol. It is rated most highly by connoisseurs.

CHAPTER 45

FLICKER

Flicker
Woodpecker's Cousin

My first memory of the flicker was when at a tender age we watched a pair excavate a dead elm branch. The elm was only a short distance directly behind our home. It was within the perimeter allowed for my wanderings, so I was able to watch the process rather continuously. As the days passed a great pile of chips accumulated at the base of the elm. The industrious pair took turns with the excavation and within a week it was about finished.

Then disaster struck. A pair of starlings proceeded to evict the flickers and set up housekeeping. I was upset and angry. I wanted to get rid of the starlings. The nest hole was about twenty-five feet from the ground so I needed help. I suggested to my mother that she become involved. She was concerned but pointed out that the drama that I had witnessed was part of nature's ways. Her philosophy was that the less we interfered, the better.

At the time I reluctantly accepted her wisdom, learning to appreciate it only in later years. But I never developed a fondness for the alien starlings.

The Northern Flicker (*Colaptes auratus*) is a member of the woodpecker tribe. It moves about on trees as do the woodpeckers. It has the undulating flight, long up-and-down swoops, as do the woodpeckers. It excavates its nesting sites as do woodpeckers. While its sound says its name, it is a definite woodpecker call.

Where it differs is in some of its feeding habits. This is the woodpecker that I see frequently on the ground. Rarely do I see the other woodpeckers working over my lawn or scratching about in the leaves under my trees. On the ground he takes various beetles and other insects that appear. What he is really after is ants.

My backyard is a sandy affair that ants find ideal. Thus, my flickers also find it ideal. At times, after the broods have left the nest, I may have six or eight of these beautiful birds devastating the ant population. They spend extended periods savoring the ant morsels until their appetite for this acid entree is satisfied.

As woodpeckers go the flicker is quite large, about eleven inches long. This means that the nest excavation will have to be quite large. The clutch runs from five to nine eggs which also necessitates a large cavity. Flickers may be induced to use bird houses if the size is adequate. In the absence of suitable tree or stub nesting sites they will do the next best thing and nest on the ground.

The flicker is the only woodpecker that displays a brown back. It also shows a very visible white rump when it flies. In flight large patches of yellow are visible under the tail and wings. This gives rise to the name Yellow-shafted or Golden-winged Woodpecker. As one moves westward across the Mississippi, the yellow changes to red to become the Red-shafted woodpecker. The sexes differ mainly in that the male sports a black cheek patch.

Several years ago I was watching a pair of flickers come and go as they fed their half-grown brood. The grasshoppers came out early that year. This pair was taking advantage of the bonanza.

As I watched through my field glasses the pair changed places every minute or so. Each time a grasshopper was clearly visible, securely pinned in the bill. In the space of a half hour or so, forty grasshoppers were persuaded to covert from insect to bird.

When he nests around human habitation our golden-winged woodpecker displays a friendliness. When on the ground he is necessarily wary, but otherwise one can come and go with little disturbance. If you are fortunate enough to have a pair nesting nearby and the starlings have not executed their tyranny, you are in for some fascinating bird watching.

CHAPTER 46

That First Pocket Knife

At a very early age I began to covet the pocket knife. An older relative always carried a well-sharpened knife which he seemed to use most of his daylight hours. There were few occasions when his three-bladed knife did not find its place.

My pleas for a knife of my own were gently put aside "until you're old enough." On occasion when I felt the overpowering need to cut, I surreptitiously used one of my mother's paring knives. I tried to be meticulous and return the knife to the knife drawer but occasionally my mother would wonder where her "black-handled paring knife" was, alerting me to a lapse.

At last came the day when I acquired one of my own. A friend of the family who worked in a cutlery factory brought a collection of seconds as a gift. A dozen or so gleaming knives lay on the table. He had brought a good assortment. He suggested to my father that I might find one useful. Carried away by the occasion my father allowed me to "take my pick." I agonized only briefly before selecting a three-bladed, stag-handled beauty. Mother's approval was not profuse, but since the deed was done she acquiesced, pointing out that should I ever cut myself, the knife would be put away "until you're old enough."

Since that time I have always carried a pocket knife. I am not ready for the day's events until my knife rests comfortably in my right hand pants pocket. Should I misplace my knife or for some other reason be without it I am uneasy and uncomfortable. When the blades are sharpened beyond effective use, or broken, or the knife becomes useless for some other reason, it is deposited in the top dresser drawer. None of these old friends are discarded. Like a good and faithful horse, it is put out to pasture.

CHAPTER 47

Brown Creeper
Woodland Acrobat

The Brown Creeper (*Certhia familiaris americana*) is pretty much a loner. I rarely ever see more than two in a given location. Although many times I do see the brown creeper together with nuthatches and chickadees.

It is an inconspicuous little brown bird that blends so well with the tree trunk on which you are most apt to find it, that movement is the only thing that gives it away. The length is about five to six inches of which half is tail. So we are dealing here with a small bird. The wings are pointed and long, the coloration, as the name suggests, is brown, drab brown.

Certhia has a long, thin, sharp bill with a downward curve. She uses this bill to gather all sorts of small insects, their larva and eggs. Most of the insects that she eats are harmful to trees so she should be welcome in any forest. The bill does not have the strength and structure of the woodpecker or nuthatch. She does not force her way into the bark but rather gathers her food from the surface or that which is lodged in the cracks and crannies.

Certhia is an acrobat on the tree trunk. With quick swooping wing beats she drops to the base of a large pine. She then works her way upward, contrary to the manner of the nuthatches. She will move sideways with a series of agile moves that almost do not seem to have been made. She spirals around as her fancy dictates. As she moves up into the branches she may follow one out, keeping largely to its underside. At last satisfied that she has gleaned the tree she drops down to another trunk to continue the process.

The brown creeper is not a shy bird. She can be approached quite closely. There are numerous recordings of nestings near or on human dwellings. But since she is so small, inconspicuous and relatively solitary she has the reputation of being timid. She does associate with other birds but with reservation.

The range of this tiny insect eater is northeastern North America from about the Dakotas and the great plains eastward and north to Hudson Bay. It is somewhat migratory in that there is a general shift in the spring and southward in the fall. I see *Certhia* during every month of the year. She brings forth her young from Canada to North Carolina.

The nest of this busy little bird is difficult to find. It usually will be found beneath the curl of bark breaking away from a dead tree. Since space requirements are minimal any loosening of bark may hide a creeper apartment. The nest itself consists of grasses, small twigs and lichens, lined with fine grasses, occasional feathers, down and the like. One writer states that the nest is always behind the bark of a balsam. The only nest I ever found was within the folds of a dead white pine. I suspect that while the birds may have preferences, they will take advantage of whatever housing is available.

She does not come to my feeder as do the nuthatches. My nuthatches have developed an appetite for sunflower seeds and suet but *Certhia* seems satisfied with her natural fare. I have read that peanut butter spread on tree trunks will be sampled by this little bird but I have not tried this addition to the menu. I'm satisfied to see her and hear her reedy, lisping call as I wander through my woods.

CHAPTER 48

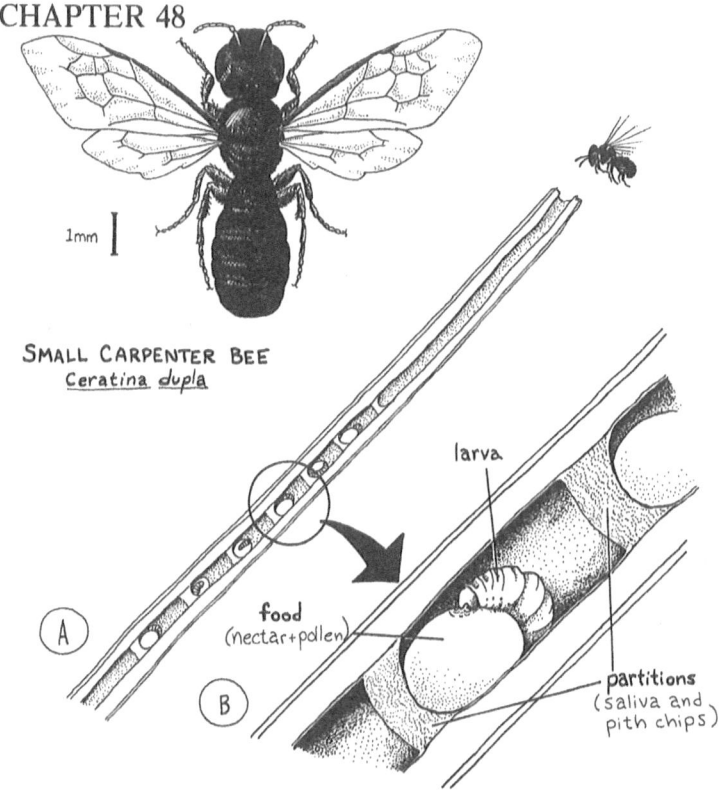

SMALL CARPENTER BEE
Ceratina dupla

(A) Nest of Ceratina in a broken Sumac branch (cut-away view)
(B) Detailed view of a single cell of a Ceratina nest

©1986 JACK NORTON

Carpenter Bee
Condo a Remarkable Structure

I was in the midst of a tangle of sumac. In front of me was what appeared to be a dead branch. Its terminal bud had been broken off. The pith had been removed. I cut off about a foot of the branch and sat down to examine it. A careful splitting revealed what must have been a monumental excavation. I was looking at the condominium of a little Carpenter Bee, *Ceratina dupla*.

The excavator of this remarkable structure was a gentle lady bee with a slender metallic blue body and multi-tinted wings.

Sometime, probably the previous May, she had found the twig that had been broken off and claimed it as her future domicile. The sumac has a soft pith which can be easily removed. And this is what she did.

The dwelling I had opened was empty except for the debris of occupancy. The bottom was packed for several inches with the refuse of living and demolishing of the apartments.

This tiny creature, only about one-quarter to three-eighths inches in length, does a prodigious job. Laboriously she removes the pith to a length of perhaps twelve inches. She has no special tools for this task. This is one reason she has to first find a twig with a broken tip and soft pithy center. In addition to sumac, the elderberry and raspberry are prime materials for these condominiums. Once she had excavated this one-eighth inch tube she proceeds to fit it for her family.

Then she lays a single egg on the pollen supply and proceeds to construct a partition sealing off the first room. This sequence is repeated until the tube is filled with tiny nurseries. My specimen had eight. Under ideal circumstances up to fourteen may be constructed.

This finished, she settles back to wait. The first egg hatches. This probably happens before the last cell is completed and occupied. The little larva feeds on the pollen provided. It grows until it is about one-quarter inch long and then pupates. To me pupation is a miraculous event. The formless white worm gradually transforms itself into a mature bee, complete with sharp eyes, legs, wings and all the other necessities for coping in the outside bee world.

The first hatchling is at the bottom of the stack. It must work its way up through all the rest of the apartments. While it has been pupating the second egg has hatched, fed and begun its pupation, and in time it starts its upward passage. Tearing away the wall that separates the apartments, each bee in turn commences its journey. The first bee has to traverse all the apartments carefully pushing the debris of its predecessors behind it. Here is a case of where being the first-born really is a disadvantage. The last bee pops its partition to find mommy who has been guarding the nest entrance all these days. She leads them off in flight.

Once she sees them on their own she returns to the condominium, gives it a thorough cleaning and starts the whole process all over again. If the last brood emerges late in the fall, its members, after feeding on pollen that they themselves gather, may return to the snug tube to spend the winter guarded by their mother.

Ceratina dupla is a true bee but very different from what we think of as a bee. When the word bee is mentioned most people think of the honey bee. A great number of people classify all wasps and hornets as bees. The true bees are more hairy than the wasps and hornets. These hairs are more branched. There are other distinguishing characteristics.

Since every living thing has its enemies, its predators, its parasites, so does the little carpenter bee. One species of wasp simply drives the carpenter bee out of her domicile appropriating it for its own use. Another wasp sneaks into the nursery when the little bee is absent and lays an egg next to the carpenter egg. When the carpenter is nearly grown the wasp egg hatches and consumes the carpenter larva.

Nature is replete with fascinating drama. To witness it, to be a part of it, all you need to do is look.

CHAPTER 49

GIANT PUFFBALL
(Calvatia gigantea)

Giant Puffball
'It Can't Get Any Better Than This'

Probably the most spectacular of our north country mushrooms, at least with respect to size, is the giant puffball. This fungus sometimes becomes enormous. I frequently find it a foot or more in diameter. One source gives the maximum as five feet high and four feet wide. I have never seen anything approaching this magnitude but have had gifts of puffballs over two feet in diameter.

As with all mushrooms, the giant puffball, *Calvatia gigantea*, is a saprophyte. That is, it does not manufacture its own food but gets its nourishment from decaying plant material. The immense body that we harvest is the fruiting body of the organism. When mature, this structure disintegrates into billions of spores. Discharged into the air, some of these spores eventually become responsible for the next generation of puffballs.

I became acquainted with the giant puffball at an early age. On mushrooming expeditions with my mother the occasional puffball would find its way into our basket. Mushrooming is like a treasure hunt. Finding a good-sized puffball insures the success of the hunt. Certainly a large puffball turning into great, gleaming slices on the kitchen table foretells of a gastronomic treasure about to be savored.

All of the various puffballs are edible. But, as is the case with many food varieties, some are better than others. The giant puffball is choice. It is better than all the rest. There is little danger, if puffball hunting, that something toxic will be consumed. A puffball is very obviously a puffball.

Having captured a puffball and sneaked it into your kitchen (this is to avoid having neighbors drop in to share your feast), your first action is to check the condition of your prize. When in excellent condition the outer skin is described as being like "white kid glove leather." It is smooth, and papery thin. If it is not smooth and gleaming white, it is past its prime. But all may not be lost.

With a large knife split the trophy lengthwise, from bottom to top. The interior should be soft but firm and very white. If you detect a slight yellowing, it is past its prime. It will not be as tasty as it should be. If very yellow, discard and try again.

You have been lucky and have harvested a prime specimen. Half lies sliced on the counter. The other half, wrapped in wax paper, lies in the refrigerator where it will keep for several days if need be. With no further preparation the quarter-inch slices may be sauteed in butter. Some like to dredge the slices in flour before sauteing. With a little salt and pepper you already have a gourmet feast.

I find that I soon get "puffballed out." That is, a meal or two satisfies my craving for the time being. My good helpmate then sautees puffball chunks with chunks of zucchini. This goes well for a meal or two. However, the pinnacle of puffball cuisine, for me, is the puffball-cheese roll that my helpmate devised.

Saute one side of a puffball slice. Turn to reciprocate on the other side. While it is sauteing place a thin slice of mild cheddar (or your favorite) on top so that it melts as the sauteing continues. Once the cheese is barely melted, quickly roll as you would a jellyroll. Serve immediately. As they say in some commercials, "It can't get any better than this."

CHAPTER 50

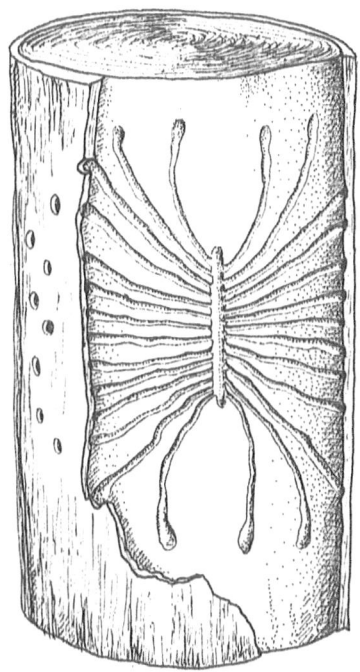

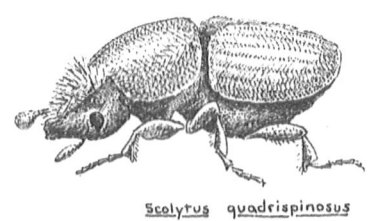

Scolytus quadrispinosus

ENGRAVER BEETLE

section of branch with bark removed to show tunnels or 'galleries'

©1984 JOHN NORTON

Engraver Beetle
One of Nature's Artists

Nature is replete with fascinating life forms. Each occupies its own particular slot. Most of the time we have little understanding of the intricacies of the arrangement. Many times a particular form works or seems to work at cross purposes to what we may believe is correct.

Nevertheless, though we may regard something as harmful, it has its place. We have not yet acquired knowledge or wisdom to appreciate the part that it plays.

One of these ambivalent forms is the engraver beetle. Worldwide, there are about 6,000 species that may fall in this category. In the United States and Canada there are perhaps 500 species that qualify. People dealing with timber and its various ramifications regard the engraver beetles as dangerous and costly pests. Those interested in art may look on the engravers as artists. Those who are intrigued by nature's diversity see the engraver as another fascinating indication of the wonderful diversity that fills our planet.

These beetles generally attack trees that are dead, dying or are weakened by some catastrophe, such as fire, flood, blowdown or drought. The male engraver beetle excavates a burrow under the bark of its target tree. It then invites a female to lay her eggs in this burrow. This is somewhat unique in the insect world for it usually is the female that takes care of home building and household duties. In one engraver species, the male cares for several females, another first in the insect world.

The eggs hatch within a few days and the interesting excavation begins. The egg chamber may be an inch or so long. Each larva begins to eat its way out from its birthplace. Each larva constructs its own dwelling, fanning out away from the central chamber.

As this slow eating migration continues, a pattern begins to develop. If you lift the bark from a dead tree you are apt to see the engraver's signature. In its early stages it may look like a many-legged spider. As the pattern develops it may take on a butterfly-like look. Identification of a particular species is often done from the pattern of the engraving.

Some of the egg galleries are marvelously designed with spaced ventilation ports leading out to just under the bark's surface. It takes two or three days for the eggs to hatch. Then the engraving starts, to continue for 30-40 days. After a pupal stage of a week or more the metamorphosed adults emerge.

In some species the adults may continue the burrowing which may alter the fringe of the pattern. In any event the adults eventually emerge and the cycle starts all over again. In our cold climate, overwintering usually occurs in the larval stage.

While most of the engraving takes place just under the bark and does little damage to the main body of wood, the serious damage occurs because of other organisms. The engraver's penetration of the tree bark provides entry portals for a host of fungi and other organisms that attack trees.

It is interesting to note that in the constant battle that goes on in the forest, some trees are able to effectively combat the engravers by drowning the larva in sap.

Recently I cut down a dead pine that had escaped my notice. It was dead to the point that the bark was loose. As I cut it up, the bark fell off, revealing the galleries of hundreds of engraver beetle larva. They had long since left their nurseries. Each pattern was a butterfly shape with a diameter of about two inches. They were evenly spaced along the trunk so that there was no overlapping. It appeared as though each colony knew when it was approaching the bounds of a neighbor. One time a friend told me that he incorporated these intricate galleries in picture frames and other items. I could see that they might add interest.

I read recently that in the tropics engraver beetles are a serious pest in lumbering operations. It seems that with some species of trees the engravers attack the newly felled tree with such rapidity and precision that frequently the logs are useless by the time they reach the saw mill. We are fortunate in the north country that this speed and precision has not been reached.

The engravers are a bane to tree lovers. They despoil good timber. But they are a part of the essential process that returns humus to the soil, the recycling of dead material. They spread disease, but they produce aesthetic works that are at least as good as those of "paint-by-chance" artist, Jackson Pollock.

CHAPTER 51

Oak Rolltop More Than A Desk— An Adventure!

My first memories of it were of its being huge. My eyes were just about at the level of the writing surface. My father's oak rolltop desk towered over me. It even surrounded me at times. The cavernous knee space had room enough that I could hide in its recesses even as my father worked at his books.

As time passed and I grew, the massiveness of the rolltop and its four-drawered companion file cabinet abated, but not its allure. My fascination for this shiny, varnished piece of furniture has never dimmed.

I suppose the initial charm was the rolltop itself. The tambour, guided by curved tracks, slid down enclosing the writing surface and the many little drawers, slots and cubby holes. A lock secured the tambour to the desktop, making its contents safe from prying little eyes and curious little hands. Actually the desk was rarely locked.

Across the back, above the writing surface, was an array of tiny drawers, vertical and horizontal slots and two larger, shallow drawers. I have always been intensely curious as to the uses the desk's designer contemplated for these spaces. My father used the small scoop-shaped drawers for stamps, rubber bands, shipping tags, mailing stickers. Each drawer held a specific collection of items that he used frequently. The various cubbyholes and slots held post cards, envelopes, blotters and other items he found necessary in his business.

In the center, under this collection, was a space that held his inkstand, a small metal elk's head, whose head contained the inkwell and whose antlers cradled his metal quill pens. Directly over the knee space was a shallow drawer that extended to the back of the desk. This was flanked on either side by four well-made drawers. On either side above these drawers was a pull-out writing surface that increased the writing area by nearly 50 percent.

I spent many happy hours, when my father was out of the office, exploring the many recesses of this fine old desk. He kept an interesting collection of small tools, curios and junk in several of the drawer compartments. I inventoried these every chance I had. Then one day while checking out the recesses under the tambour, I found two secret drawers.

They were long, narrow and shallow. They could not hold much of substance. However, I imagined that they might, at one time, have held a rolled up map of buried treasure, tightly folded secret government documents, a spy's report. I was almost beside myself with excitement trying to contain the discovery of this provocative secret.

I wanted to share the discovery with my father. The disclosure, however, would reveal the fact that I played with his desk. I had never been expressly forbidden to explore his desk but there was a kind of unspoken rule that his business papers should not be touched. Disclosure might mean that I would never again sit in his highbacked, swivel chair and steer the solid oaken ship through the seven seas. I might never again drive the sturdy covered wagon, with its rolltop, across the plains, floating it across swollen rivers, defeating prairie fires, storms and of course, Indians.

But I had to do it. One day with subdued excitement, I pointed out the two secret hiding places. I carefully pulled the drawers out and laid them before his eyes. I was exploding with excitement. I never really knew whether or not he had been aware of the drawers before my disclosure.

If he knew, he gave no sign. He marveled at my discovery. He examined each of the tiny compartments carefully. He wondered at my skills of discovery. I suggested that the secret should be revealed to no one and he agreed.

Eventually I acquired the desk and the filing cabinet. It was decided to strip and refinish the desk. This meant disassembly. It also meant that since it would be torn apart that the tambour should be repaired as the ancient cloth backing was falling apart.

Disassembly was relatively simple. The desk was designed to last. The designer realized that every 50 to 75 years it would need refinishing and designed it so that it could be taken apart easily. At last we had it apart. The rounded slats were stripped, refinished and glued to a new sturdy cloth backing. The desk top with all its compartments stood separately, gleaming in its new coat of varnish.

The writing top was removed to reveal a locking mechanism that secured the side drawers whenever the tambour was pulled down. Sometime, ages ago, it had broken. We had never realized that the entire desk could be secured. With the locking mechanism repaired and all the stripping and revarnishing accomplished, the desk stood restored to some of its original grandeur.

It now occupies a place in my office. At least once a day I sit before it. Sometimes I do some work. Sometimes I reminisce, guiding the sturdy ship around the horn to the South Seas, or drive the rolltop wagon into a circle with other wagons in the train. It never was nor ever will be just a desk.

CHAPTER 52

House Wren
Ruins Predictions

Everyone knows the House Wren. I thought I did too. But as time goes on and I see more and more of him I'm less and less sure. This dynamic little bundle of aggressive feathers has his habits and is predictable to a considerable extent. But just as I think I have him figured out he breaks his habit. He does a turn-around and ruins my predictions.

When I first moved into my present home I wanted to provide substantial bird housing. I constructed about a dozen apartments and placed them around my yard. I hoped to attract tree swallows, bluebirds and wrens. I had hanging homes, bungalows on posts, chalets fastened to tree trunks. My yard boasted an abundance of possible bird dwellings. Tree swallows were the first to arrive and inspect the houses. A bluebird appeared (its mate a day after) and selected a residence. Things seemed to be going according to plan.

The wren was the last to arrive. He inspected the domiciles and proceeded to evict the bluebirds. The remaining homes he attempted to fill with twigs. At the same time there was conflict with the tree swallows. One pair remained steadfast but the other could not stand the onslaught. I was left with a great quantity of twigs stashed around the yard, a pair of tree swallows and a pair of wrens. Some time later I discovered that there were two pairs of wrens located as far apart as my bird residential organization would permit.

The wren will nest in just about any cavity. Its nest is a dense framework of twigs lined with grasses, down and feathers. Six to eight eggs comprise the clutch. Wrens live almost exclusively on insects. Providing worms, flies and bugs for six or eight hungry mouths keeps the parents busy. There is a steady stream of wrens in and out of the nest after the eggs are hatched.

House Wrens breed from New Brunswick to Ontario, south to the mid-Atlantic states and winter in the Gulf states. They are brown colored, smaller than sparrows and have the wren characteristic of cocking their tails over their backs. The house wren song is a bubbling, effervescent melody that sings of exuberance, of the incomparable joy of being alive.

A few years ago, armed with a chainsaw and a pile of pine logs, I devised a method for mass-producing a rustic birdhouse. It was easily sawed and assembled. In my fit of enthusiasm I produced more than I could use. I replaced the old birdhouses, put my product in new locations, and still had a surplus. These half dozen I stored on a shelf in my garage.

During the summer I rarely close my garage doors. One day I noticed a wren fly out of the garage. It soon became apparent that a pair of wrens was inspecting the condominiums lined up on the back shelf. One was selected and a brood produced. The other apartments were filled with twigs. Later in the season a second brood was produced in a different residence. None of the other birdhouses I so carefully placed around my yard housed a wren that year.

Like many small individuals the wren makes up for his lack of size by being loud and aggressive. Small dog breeds, the Pekinese, the Chihuahua, seem to be far more loud and aggressive than their size would warrant. This is a pattern I seem to notice from time to time within the human species also.

Despite his aggressive tendencies, despite his inability to live with other bird species around my yard, I am very fond of the house wren. He more than pays his way with the cabbage worms he eats from my garden. He stimulates me with his exhilarating concerts. He sets an example and reminds me that life is a joy, very much worth living.

CHAPTER 53

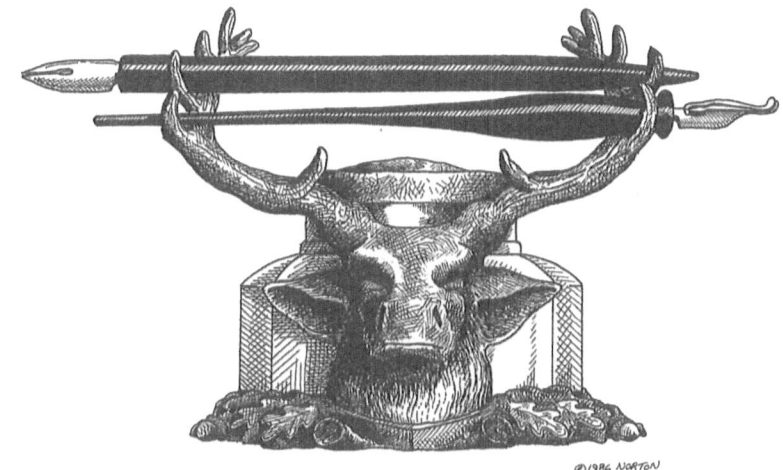

Sir Elk, the Penstand
We Go Back a Long Way

My father's rolltop oak desk had a recess at the back under its many cubbyholes. Ensconced in this recess rested his elk head pen stand. Like a king on his throne, the elk stared sternly out at me, his antlers festooned with several wooden penholders with metal pen points. My eyes, barely desktop high, stared back. There was, and still is, I think, the element of mutual admiration.

Cast out of white metal, Sir Elk features two long antler beams that sweep majestically back. The first two antler points project forward at a slight upward angle. Eight other points project upward, four from each beam. This arrangement can cradle a half dozen or more penholders. Its nostrils are flared and its ears angled slightly forward as if scenting the air and listening carefully to the small boy who stands before it.

Nestled behind the head, between the antlers, is a heavy glass ink well. It is covered by a thin metal cover that has some sort of coat of arms design pressed in its top. The cap is somewhat dented and bears a few ink stains. The glass well has not held ink for many years. But inside are dry, powdery, blue splotches, traces of the ink it held long ago. The majestic elk head and its sweeping antlers also show ink stains. At times I am tempted to clean up this regal artifact, to eradicate the ink stains and bring back the original shiny luster.

Barely tall enough to see across the blotter that covered the desk top, I first encountered its unyielding gaze at eye level. In my mind's eye I fix on the stern eyes, the flaring nostrils, the rack loaded with pens. The splashes of blue ink are there. It is an old friend. The ink stains compare to combat wounds. They recount a history. They should not be removed.

So the dusty, ink stained, somewhat grimy, pen stand sits in its accustomed place. Several old wooden penholders with their metal penpoints rest on the antlers. There is no danger of its being robbed of its heritage. The stern gaze fixes mine. The flaring nostrils sniff my scent. The ears almost twitch as they catch the whispers of my breathing. Sir Elk and I go back a long way. He reminds me of my past. It is a strong link that helps me cope.

CHAPTER 54

Ape-Man Trolley
Tremendous Fun

In my early youth I saw a movie that depicted the adventures of a voluntary castaway on a desert tropical island. One of his intriguing, but most improbable, accomplishments was the construction of a transportation system that I called the "Ape-man trolley." Using this device he rode in a woven cage through the jungle, bringing food and other necessities to his elaborate dwelling.

My imagination was piqued. I envisioned something of the sort through the trees of our backyard. The next day I began to scrounge to see what materials were available for my endeavor. A length of rope and at least one pulley were minimum requirements.

I finally found a long piece of old rope and, after some diligent searching, discovered an old hay pulley in a box of old tools.

Now, settling on a site was the next problem. There was a large, familiar, well-branched black cherry in which I had built several tree houses. Across a small gully were a number of smaller trees. This seemed ideal.

It took a considerable amount of hauling and climbing but at last the rope was secured from a high branch in my cherry to the trunk of a small elm across the gully. I was about to launch the first aerial trolley in Lewis County when I accidentally let go of the pulley which made the historic trip by itself. It came to rest in the center of the rope, suspended several feet above my reach directly over the gully.

This of course meant that to get the pulley back I had to dismantle my tramway. It also suggested that unless some modifications were made I would have to dismantle and "remantle" the line after each ride. So a length of stout cord was obtained. With one end tied to the pulley and the other secured to the cherry branch the pulley could now be pulled back to the launch platform after each ride.

The first ride was not what I had expected. Instead of an exhilarating ride, waving as I passed mile after mile through the jungle, I was airborne for but a few seconds before I crashed into the far bank of the gully. My rope hung too low. It had too much slack.

I selected another small elm farther away, readjusted the slack, climbed back up the cherry, pulled the pulley back up to the launch platform and was ready for the second historic try.

The second ride was appreciably longer. I was able to distinguish several trees as I flashed across the gully before I "splatted" belly first against the trunk of the terminal elm.

After I recovered my breath, which was spread out all over the gully, it became apparent that some modifications were in order if I was to survive this endeavor.

A maple with a strong branch well above the ground seemed to be the answer.

I tied the "end of the line" portion of my rope securely to this branch, well out from the trunk. Then the laborious process of climbing back up the cherry, pulling the pulley back across the gully got me in position for the third try.

I was by now an experienced "tramonaut." My launch was good. The trip was exciting. As I approached the terminus I was able to let go of the pulley, drop lightly to the ground with a minimum of colliding and a modicum of dignity.

The ape-man trolley was a success!

It still needed some adjustments, but I made trip after trip throughout the rest of the afternoon.

On the bottom of the pulley was a large hook that I had to grasp with both hands as I swung through the air. I had envisioned a car to ride my cable. After several days of experimentation I fashioned a platform that hung from the pulley's hook. It was rather small and not like the cage in the movie. But I was short of material. Nevertheless it was large enough to hold me.

I would not stand waving at the countryside as I brought a load of bananas and coconuts down the mountain but at least I would not have to hang on for dear life.

My previous experience suggested that I allow the cable car to make its maiden trip alone. This I did and discovered that there were more adjustments that needed to be made. It also brought to mind that unless I could somehow quickly leave the vehicle as it reached its downhill terminus I might roll backward and end up suspended over the gully. This is one of my earlist recollections of profiting from my own experience.

Finally I had to abandon the cage. As it approached the end of the trip it would slowly twist on its suspensions.

Sometimes this would present me back-first, unable to jump off no matter what modifications I tried. In the end I settled on a stirrup of rope. The length was adjusted so that with one foot in the stirrup and hanging on to the pulley hook with one hand (to insure that I would face the right direction for the touchdown) I could ride with abandon.

Now I could wave to the jungle residents as I passed by overhead, recklessly dangling from the stirrup, shouting in triumph. The nearly five-second trip seemed almost as good as the movie version. My Ape-man trolley occupied me most of the rest of the summer.

As the time for school approached I disassembled my creation. The neatly coiled rope was deposited in a box, the pulley nestled within its coils. The stirrup, now modified with the toe of an old boot secured in the bottom loop to hold my foot, together with the other parts of my tramway were folded on top.

The box was put away to await the glories of the next summer.

But somehow during the following year I changed. Perhaps I matured a little. Maybe my priorities changed. I never did resurrect the ape-man trolley.

I went on to other things.

CHAPTER 55

AMERICAN BITTERN

Mud Hen
Thunder Pumper

"There's a Mud hen, in that tall grass." I was about ten or twelve. We were bullhead fishing on the Black River at the outlet of a drainage ditch. In the tall grass across the ditch was this "Mud hen" which I could not see. We had walked along the Black River flats to the ditch, baited our lines and had started the serious business of bullhead fishing.

The mud hen had watched this procedure with its head pointed toward the sky, secure in its camouflage. I searched the opposite bank of the ditch but try as I would I could not see this strangely named creature. This has occurred many times since. The thunder pumper has superb camouflage. He can be but a few feet away and be all but invisible.

The American bittern (*Botaurus lentiginous*) is a member of the heron family. This drab bird ranges from 24 to 36 inches in length. A resident of marshes and swamps he can frequently be found feeding in meadows. The mixed brown, black and white on his back and the streaked yellowish colors below make for startingly good concealment.

This marsh bird breeds from the Gulf of Mexico north to Southern Canada. It winters in the Gulf states, sometimes as far north as the mid-Atlantic latitudes. Its flight is slow and deliberate. It appears to be labored but in fact is strong and powerful. It performs no aerial acrobatics but its measured strokes will quickly move it across the marsh from your sight.

Probably the most remarkable feature of this marsh citizen is the sound that it makes. It can hardly be called a song. One source compares it to the sound made by the old fashioned wood pump as it sucks and thumps water. Thunder pumper is a good description. Another source compares the sound to that produced when a stake is driven into the ground. This gives rise to the apt name, stake driver. This sound seems more apparent when its maker is at some distance.

However you describe it, it is unique. It is difficult to judge the direction of the source as well as its distance. Some peculiar sound property makes this noise seem to come from every direction as well as from nowhere. It will seem to be nearby when it is at a considerable distance and far-off when the bird is close by in the rushes.

My marsh has a vantage point which allows me to look down on it from a height. I have spent many hours searching for the thunder pumper as he executes his tympany below. Field glasses seem to be of little help. I locate him only when he moves. His sound has a camouflage all its own and defeats me every time.

Bog bull (another descriptive name) builds his sloppy, loose nest of rushes on ground above the water. Since my marsh is subject to late spring Black River floods these nests are often flooded out. Three to five eggs will be carefully incubated. When on the nest the American bittern is most difficult to see.

The diet is varied. Anything of swallowable size that can be caught by the efficient swift bill will contribute to the meal. Thus, fish, frogs, snakes, salamanders, grasshoppers, crayfish, and mice find themselves listed on the menu. During August when the grasshopper population is high I have watched the thunder pumper feast in unmowed meadows. The tall grass gives concealment. The grasshoppers give nourishment. The thunder pumper gives me entertainment.

CHAPTER 56

QUEEN ANNE'S LACE

©1984 JOHN NURTON

Queen Anne's Lace
'Weed' is Delicately Beautiful

    I was probably about ten. We were at the edge of a field that from a distance appeared almost white. It was sometime in late summer or early fall. My mother was trying to point out the beauty of the flower that gave the field its wash of white. I was not impressed.
    To be beautiful, a flower had to be large and have color. Tulips, lilies and sunflowers were my idea of beautiful. To be sure, this white umbrella-shaped flower was large. We found

132

some that were four to five inches across but I remained unimpressed. I was even less thrilled when she told me its name, Queen Anne's Lace. A second name, wild carrot, did nothing to stimulate my interest.

This alien biennial is found throughout the country from coast to coast, but is most common along the Eastern borders. Probably native to Asia it migrated through Europe and eventually came to America with the colonists. It grows well in dry abandoned fields and roadsides. It is from the twenty or so species in this genus that our present day carrots have descended.

With age comes a modicum of maturity. Gradually I accumulated snatches of acumen. Somewhere along the line I began to see the beauty in this prolific weed. Color or size no longer were requirements for beauty in a flower. Form and shape contributed elegance and thus, beauty. I began to see a whole new world.

This biennial may reach three feet in height. If mowed its stems will get successively shorter but it will persist. It has attractive, lacy, slender leaves that are doubly, sometimes triply, compounded. The tip of the stalk displays the flower which is a complex umbel (many single flower stalks originating from the same point) radiating outward and upward. This ultimately forms a sort of flat-topped umbrella.

In the center of this lacy platform is a very dark purple, almost black, spot of tiny flowers. Several individuals have told me of finding blossoms that were pink rather then white. Apparently the many tiny flowers that comprise the blossom are abundantly supplied with nectar as it is difficult to find one that does not have its complement of bees, butterflies and other insects. Since the stalks are tall and tough, the ripe fruit is frequently found above the winter's snow.

The seeds will persist for several years. The roots are strong and deep. Thus, once your yard becomes infested, eradication is difficult. Perhaps you should gracefully give in and just enjoy the delicate beauty of this ubiquitous weed.

CHAPTER 57

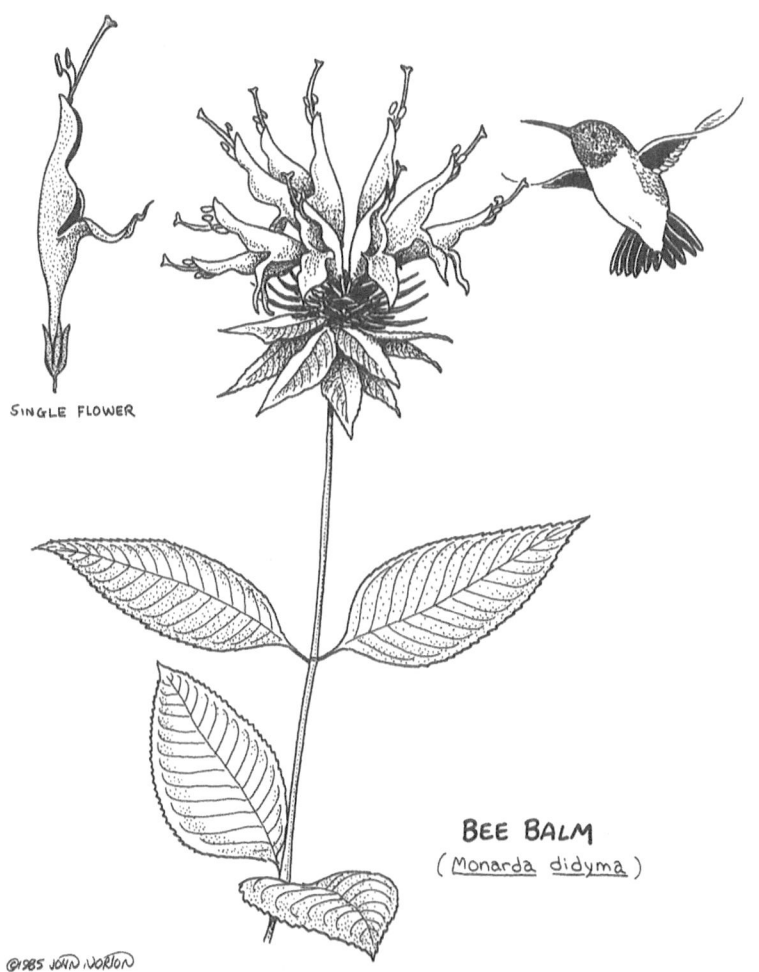

Bee Balm
Delightful Memory

    For many years my mother's perennial garden had a clump of brilliant red flowers. In my early years I was very partial to red, so this clump was an instant favorite. For me, another attraction to this plant was its name, Bee Balm, or Oswego Tea.
    It was easy to see why it was called Bee Balm as its flowers had a constant stream of visiting bees. Its other name, Oswego Tea,

appears to come from the fact that the Oswego Indians taught the early settlers to make a medicinal tea from the leaves and blossoms of this plant.

The square-stemmed bee balm, *Monarda didyma*, is a mint. It likes rich, moist soil. Most of the clumps that I find are along stream beds. It grows well in shade and if conditions are right may produce a stalk of five feet or more. It spreads by means of undergound runners. Thus a single plant may spread into a clump several feet across in two or three years.

Shortly after World War II, I was fishing a small trout stream that ran through a narrow valley. I gradually became aware of a scent that was familiar but which I could not identify. As I worked upstream the scent became stronger. I was filled with a warm comfortable feeling. A nostalgic wave ran over me as my mother's perennial garden flashed into my mind's eye. Suddenly I knew the source of the scent.

I rounded a turn in the narrow valley to come upon several large masses of the brilliant red of the bee balm. Fishing stopped for the day. I sat on a grassy slope and soaked in the sight, scent and the sound, (for the flowers were loaded with bees and butterflies and hummingbirds) of this marvelous flower. I came home with an empty fish basket but from a most successful fishing trip.

There are over a dozen Monards in North America. Their blooms run a wide range of colors from white through red. A species, *Monarda fistulosa*, called Wild Bergamot, has a lilac tint and a slightly more Northern range than does bee balm. Both species are found in the North Country. This species will thrive on drier soil than will the bee balm.

In the early colonial days many North American plants were sent back to Europe. The spectacular pom-pom of red tubular flowers found instant favor and soon bee balm was growing all over Europe. Plant breeders have produced a number of delightful cultivars. While I cannot deny their beauty I must favor the deep, brilliant massive red of the clump of Oswego Tea that graced my mother's perennial garden, that perfumed the air around the cool of a trout stream, that even today evokes warm, pleasant feelings when I catch its scent.

CHAPTER 58

BLUE-EYED-GRASS

'Blue-Eyed' Grass
Spurs Appreciation

I recall with fondness a gently sloping bank near the Black River not far from my home. This grassy slope contained an interesting flower that was one of the first of the smaller flowers to take my fancy. Well above flood waters, this green mat looked out over the Black River. I was about ten years old. It was a pleasant place to sit and watch the swirling waters pass by.

Usually when I visited this spot my gaze was directed to the river. But one day my attention was turned to the green rug on which I was lying. Scattered through the grasses was a stiff, flat-stemmed plant that displayed a very pretty blue-violet flower at its tip.

I picked a small bouquet and took them to my mother. She told me that these flowers were called blue grass flower or blue-eyed grass and suggested that it would probably be better if I did not pick the flowers but rather allowed them to go to seed and produce more plants. She pointed out that in picking the flower I had also picked most of the leaves which might weaken, if not kill the plant.

The species which I picked was probably *Sisyrinchium montanum*, one of nine species that are supposed to be in the north country. Two of these species are white rather than blue. In ideal locations they can reach two feet in height. My specimens were barely eight inches tall. Some species have branched stems and display several flowers. My species had a single wide, flat stem. These grass flowers belong to the Iris family. They have a wide range: from southern Canada, the Lake states, south in mountainous areas, to Virginia.

The relatively inconspicuous blossoms have six petals, each bearing a tiny point. Almost any undisturbed moist meadow will contain some of these delightful flowers. The blooming period is May through July.

I suggested that it would be nice to have some of these flowers on our river bank. My mother was never too keen on removing wildflowers from their natural settings. Probably with the idea of stimulating my plant education, she agreed that I might transplant a few if the meadow had a good supply.

So, armed with a trowel, a large pail and very detailed information, I set forth. I returned with six plants, each with a large ball of earth. They were carefully transplanted in an open spot on our river bank. The soil was carefully firmed around the roots. I watered them carefully and was restrained from fertilizing them. My watchful mentor suggested that at this stage fertilizer might do more harm than good.

So with the help of the Blue-eyed Grass I learned something about plant care, conservation, and gained an appreciation of the beauty of the small flower.

www.ingramcontent.com/pod-product-compliance
Lightning Source LLC
Chambersburg PA
CBHW031422290426
44110CB00011B/487